Just a Bunch of Girls
Feminist Approaches
to Schooling

Edited by

GABY WEINER

OPEN UNIVERSITY PRESS

Milton Keynes · *Philadelphia*

The Open University Press
12 Cofferidge Close
Stony Stratford
Milton Keynes MK11 1BY, England
and
242 Cherry Street
Philadelphia, PA 19106, USA

First published 1985   Reprinted 1986, 1987, 1989

British Library Cataloguing in Publication Data

Just a bunch of girls: feminist approaches
to schooling.—(Gender and education)
1. Women—Education—Great Britain
I. Weiner, Gaby   II. Series
376'.941   LC2042

ISBN 0–335–15025–X

Library of Congress Cataloging in Publication Data

Just a bunch of girls.
    Bibliography: p.
    Includes index.
    1. Sex discrimination in education—Great Britain—
Addresses, essays, lectures.   2. Educational equal-
ization—Great Britain—Addresses, essays, lectures.
3. Women—Education—Great Britain—Addresses,
essays, lectures. 4. Feminism—Great Britain—
Addresses, essays, lectures. I. Weiner, Gaby.
LC212.83.G7J87 1985   370.19'345   84–22736

ISBN 0–335–15025–X (pbk.)

Text Design by Clarke Williams

Typeset by S & S Press, Abingdon, Oxfordshire
Printed in Great Britain by
M. & A. Thomson Litho Limited,
East Kilbride, Scotland

CONTENTS

SERIES EDITOR'S INTRODUCTION

In the period since the mid-1970s issues about gender and education have begun to receive considerable attention from researchers and educationists. Much of the work done has been of necessity exploratory and sometimes very descriptive, focusing on the identification of problems rather than on the formulation of positive strategies. Furthermore although race and education has also become a major area of debate and concern, it has been rare to find the two issues of racism and sexism discussed side by side. Rather a tradition of treating race and gender as separate social divisions has established itself, with little consideration given to the inter relationships between gender and race.

This book, the second in the *Gender and Education* series, takes a step forward therefore in two directions. First it includes in its comprehensive coverage of issues in the education of girls, a whole section of good practice and positive strategies, and also puts forward many new ideas and suggestions for future reforms and changes. Secondly, it treats race and gender as related rather than separate issues, and several contributors raise questions about how racism and sexism interrelate. The collection also adds valuable material to already existing work on how girls themselves experience their schooling, and broaches the critical and often neglected or understated subject of sexual harassment in schools. Furthermore it deals with primary, secondary and nursery sectors. In her introduction, Gaby Weiner points out the relevance of understanding the two different approaches to the eradication of sexism from schooling; the 'equal opportunities' perspective which concentrates on access to existing organizational structures and curriculum, and the more radical 'anti-sexist' perspective which has homed-in on the development of new structures and curricula.

Although the book makes clear that both approaches can learn from each other, and that they are not mutually exclusive, it is also evident that the 'equal opportunities' approach may fail to recognize or deal adequately with male–female power relations and their connections to gender inequalities. The existence of dual approaches to sexism in education is paralleled by a similar duality in the related area of race and education, where proponents are divided between the liberal 'multicultural education' perspective and the more radical 'anti-racist education' perspective. It is hoped that *Just a Bunch of Girls* will help teachers, parents and other readers to become aware of the derivations, implications and importance of different approaches, whilst offering a wealth of empirical detail and positive help to those who wish to change the schooling of girls, from whatever perspective. It will also provide further documentation and a source of ideas (in sections I and III) for those who found the first book in the series, *Co-education Reconsidered* a useful starting point for identifying some of the issues implicated in educational policies and processes involving the schooling of girls. In addition, for girls and women who themselves are aware of the extent to which sexism pervades their education, chapters 5–8 provide a hitherto largely hidden account of what it is like to be a girl in a modern school, nearly a decade after the passage of the Sex Discrimination Act. And for those who believe that legislation alone can and does evoke change, the struggles and experiences of the women and girls recorded here actually demonstrate that legislation can only play a small part in bringing about new developments; and that what is still very much required are strong personal commitment, positive policies and strategies for overcoming sexism and racism at all levels of the education system, and clear views about why and how these social divisions permeate so much of our schooling system. With its clear, readable but challenging, and radical style and content, this book has much to offer readers concerned about girls' education, whatever their starting point or present state of knowledge.

Rosemary Deem

ACKNOWLEDGEMENTS

I should like to thank the following people for their help with this book: Yvonne Beecham, Rosemary Deem, Doris Frederick, Sheila Gilks, Margherita Rendel, Hazel Taylor, the Weiners and Sheridan Welsh.

LIST OF CONTRIBUTORS

The **Anti-Sexist Working Party** is made up of classroom teachers living and working in London. The members of the group all share a common commitment to feminism and to challenging sexism and racism in primary schools. They have been together for three years but feel that they have only just begun.

Battersea County Women's Group is made up of women who either taught or are still teaching at Battersea County School, a mixed inner-city comprehensive. They are all committed feminists who, at the time of writing, were also members of the school's anti-sexist working party. They represent four different subject departments; social studies, mathematics, art and careers.

Avtar Brah is a lecturer at the Open University. She previously worked as a researcher at the Universities of Bristol and Leicester and is active in the black women's movement.

Naima Browne has taught for several years in an inner London nursery and is now a member of the Bilingual Under Fives Project Team which involves advising nursery teachers on aspects of bilingualism. She has organised and run workshops for interested nursery and infant teachers on anti- and non-sexist teaching strategies.

Marina Foster is a black South African teacher who came to the UK in 1969. She studied at several British universities as a United Nations Fellow (sic) and worked at the Centre of Urban Educational Studies in ILEA for ten years. She is now a member of the Racial Equality in Education Team in Berkshire. She was on the editorial committee of the ILEA journal *The Multi-Ethnic Education Review* and is currently an editorial member of the journal *Dragon's Teeth*.

Pauline France has been a teacher in nursery, infant and junior schools in London and for five years was an advisory teacher at ILEA's Centre for Urban Educational Studies. During this time she directed an action research project focusing on the development of approaches and materials which support the language and learning of bilingual under fives in the nursery classroom.

Lesley Holly currently works at the Open University as a researcher. She lives in Cambridge with her three children. It is their experiences in schools which provides the impetus for her work on education.

Carol Jones is a white, working class Revolutionary Feminist who has campaigned against male violence for a number of years. She is currently working with other women to set up refugees for young women who are incest survivors. She has worked in London for the last six years as a teacher and part-time youth worker and has recently joined a Girl's Project.

Val Millman is a teacher living and working in Coventry. Through her work in career's guidance and on vocational projects, she is exploring ways of helping girls to achieve personal and economic independence, despite the realities of low pay and recession.

Rehana Minhas was born in Uganda and came to Britain in 1972. She was active in socialist politics throughout her time as secondary teacher in Leeds and London and has recently started work as the Divisional Coordinator for Multi-Ethnic Education in Hackney.

Frankie Ord is an Australian who has taught in a number of London comprehensives for six years. At present she is head of English, a teacher governor and a member of the school anti-sexist and anti-racist working groups. She was also a past chair-person of the Staff Association of Brondesbury and Kilburn, which supported many of the earliest feminist initiatives within the school.

Jane Quigley is an Australian who has taught in a variety of inner London comprehensives for the past eight years. She currently holds the posts of deputy head of English and deputy head of the first and second years at Brondesbury and Kilburn and was a convenor of the school's anti-sexist working party. She is also a teacher governor and has been awarded a year's leave of absence to investigate feminist initiatives in Australian schools.

Kathryn Riley is currently completing some research on the schooling of black girls in inner South London, where she worked as a teacher for eight years. She is now Women's Equality Officer for the London Borough of Greenwich and lives in Brixton. She has been active in Labour Party politics for many years.

Leila Suleiman (*pseudonym*) is Sue Suleiman's daughter and is currently studying for her A-levels at a college of Further Education.

Susan Suleiman (*pseudonym*) is from a working class family with English, Jewish, Scottish, Greek, Armenian and Turkish connections. She is currently employed in local government on the construction/design side and is a feminist, a socialist and a trade unionist (NALGO). She was active in her branch equal rights sub-committee from 1975–84 and is currently a governor of an ILEA boys maladjusted boarding school.

Gaby Weiner has worked in education since 1972 as a primary teacher, as a researcher, as a worker on a Youth Opportunities Scheme, and in curriculum development at the Schools Council. She is now working on how to get issues of race and gender into mainstream educational courses at the Open University.

SECTION 1

Some Important Issues Highlighted

CHAPTER 1

Equal Opportunities, Feminism and Girls' Education: Introduction

GABY WEINER

This book is not a treatise on equality of opportunity or an examination of educational sex differences: it is an account of the schooling experiences of girls and women in the 1980s. It focuses on the recent struggles of feminist teachers, parents and pupils to get issues of girls' education on the schooling agenda. It is a celebration of their commitment to educational improvement. And it is also a candid account of the setbacks they have encountered in the face of an often entrenched education system.

The twelve articles in this book cover the whole range of schooling; from the nursery to secondary school and the links between school and work. They also consider aspects of education that have long been the concern of feminists eg. racism, sexual harassment, the relationship between race, class and gender, and how effectively to support girls.

Also mentioned in this volume, and much discussed at planning meetings prior to its publication, is the tension between feminist explanations of sexual divisions in schooling and the rationale behind current 'equal opportunities' thinking. It is this last issue which is the focus of this chapter.

The legal foundations of sex equality in this country have been provided by the Equal Pay and Sex Discrimination Acts. When the Sex Discrimination Act (1975) was passed, it was agreed (contrary to the advice of certain groups) that education should be included within its scope (Weiner, 1976). Yet in the first ten years of the Act not one complaint of educational discrimination has been upheld, though the Equal Opportunities Commission (EOC) has sometimes dealt with complaints 'behind the scenes'.[1] This is not to say that there is no sex discrimination in education but, rather, that the existing legislation has proved ineffective in providing a basis for change in our schools.

Meanwhile schools continue to operate outside the law. For instance, where 11+ selection still survives, different pass rates are set to equalize admissions to grammar school.[2] However the EOC, established to monitor the Sex Discrimination Act, considers that the use of different pass rates for girls and boys is a discriminatory practice and that identical tests should be used for both sexes (EOC, 1983, p. 4).

The EOC also regards as discriminatory the use of gender as a criterion for the allocation of pupils to subjects eg. directing girls towards child care or home economics, or boys to technical drawing or metalwork (EOC, 1979). Yet these practices also still survive (EOC, 1982, p. 21–2).

Despite (or perhaps, because of) the apparent ineffectiveness of the legislation, the equality of girls' education has become an important issue among an increasing number of local education authorities, teachers and parents (Millman & Weiner, 1984). Hence, examination results have been scrutinized, text books and reading schemes have been revised and class registers have been 'de-sexed'. Alongside these, more general discussion has continued about the capacity of schools to widen pupil opportunity at a time when society itself is rapidly running out of opportunities, especially for the young. So, why, then, the concern?

Interest in the development of anti-sexist (and anti-racist) practice in schools has its origins in the sustained economic and educational growth of the 1960s and 1970s. At that time it seemed that the interests of the legislators on the one hand, and activist teachers and parents, on the other, were beginning to converge. To paraphrase the rhetoric of the day, the country needed more skilled labour and government was prepared to use the law-courts to release disadvantaged groups from the constraints of prejudice and the segmented labour market.

As the country moved into recession and unemployment became a regular feature of daily life, government grew less interested in equality issues – the rhetoric remained but funds, never substantial, were progressively withdrawn.[3] Moreover a particular brand of conservative ideology celebrating domesticity and motherhood began to gain popularity (Campbell, 1984a).

However, teachers (and some parents) have continued to apply pressure for an improvement in girls' education since they, particularly, have been constantly reminded that girls still receive an unfair educational deal.[4]

At the end of the 1970s important changes were initiated by feminist teachers, who exploited the gap between rhetoric and reality revealed by the educational implications of the Sex Discrimination Act (Cornbleet & Libovitch, 1983). If the Sex Discrimination Act was the official commitment to making society more equal, what, they asked, were schools doing to implement the spirit of the legislation?[5]

They expressed their concern about sexism at staff meetings; they wrote reports about discrimination in the content and organization of the school curriculum; they wrote critical commentaries about the white, middle-class male domination of school hierarchies; and, not least, they tried to support girls at every level of schooling.

For their endeavours, they drew gratitude from female pupils and teachers but indifference and, in some cases, hostility from some of their male colleagues. The latter often reacted either by stoutly defending their acceptance of the traditional role of women as primarily that of home-maker and child carer – or by simply refusing to take any discussion of the issues seriously.

Nevertheless feminist teachers began to increase their influence – and also keep exhaustion at bay – by forming their own school support groups and/or joining local women's groups such as the London Women's Education Group and the Manchester and Sheffield Women and Education Groups (see appendix for details).

They also began to exert pressure on senior school management and local authorities for the review of policies on equal opportunity and, more urgently, for financial support for the development of non-sexist (and non-racist) curricular resources.

Within Inner London Education Authority (ILEA) they had some success in gaining official support to the extent that several teachers were seconded to local and national research and development projects and in-service courses on sex-differentiation were allowed to take place. Elsewhere, though, progress was patchy and feminists had generally to rely on their own resources and the growing national feminist network.

By the early 1980s, then, a number of schools had devised their own equal opportunities policies, posts of responsibility had been created at school level, national projects were under way (eg. the *Schools Council Sex Differentiation Project* and the EOC/SSRC funded *Girls into Science and Technology* (GIST)); and of considerable importance, some newly elected Labour councils had become actively committed to the elimination of educational disadvantage. In ILEA, for instance, the commitment was to eliminating disadvantage not only on the basis of gender but also of race and class (ILEA, 1981).

As a consequence, equal opportunities related to race and gender now went 'mainstream' (at least in certain education authorities) and senior educational management was directed towards encouraging the implementation of equal opportunities practice in schools.

At this point, five or more years from the first contemporary feminist initiatives, many of the earlier activists had withdrawn from the campaign – exhausted and unrewarded – though they still continued to work at classroom level.

The posts now created by local authorities to extend and implement equality of opportunity tended, with some notable exceptions, to go to 'second wave' activists; that is to career teachers within the existing school power structure rather than to the pioneering and radical teachers who had first taken action.

These new appointments had important consequences for the policies eventually adopted. Although both these groups, 'mainstream' and 'grassroots', agreed that education and schooling continued still to be dominated by white, middle-class males, their approaches to challenging sexism and sex discrimination in schools were based on entirely different rationales. The most acceptable view (to local education authorities and the DES) tended to focus on *equal opportunities* ie. equality of access for both girls and boys, to existing educational benefits; whereas the more radical *anti-sexist* approach concentrated on the development of a girl-centred education.

Because these two approaches reflected a clear difference of opinion about the identification of and the solution to sexual divisions in schooling and therefore had important consequences for the school initiatives eventually undertaken, I wish now to consider each of them in more detail.

Equality of opportunity – what's in it for girls?

Education has long been one of the most decisive of our life's chances, the key to equal opportunity and the ladder to advancement, since men first learnt that literacy and communication in the hands of a few meant power, government and control of many. Without education and especially without equal educational experiences or skill or qualifications, men and women alike of certain classes and social groups have over the years been condemned to inferior lives in their personal development, in their choice of work, as citizens, and in their power to influence government, leadership and the national decisions which affect their local lives.

(Byrne E., *Women and Education*, Tavistock, 1978, p. 14)

The concept of equality of opportunity was first given official recognition in the 1944 Education Act though since then our interpretation of its meaning has undergone substantial alteration. It was then held that pupils were to be given the opportunity to realize their full potential – as predicted by psychological tests of attainment and intelligence.

In the 1950s and 1960s, however, social scientists began to recognise a class bias in the education system. They discovered that working-class children were much less likely to receive the full benefits of a grammar school education than middle-class children of the same measured potential. A broader interpretation of equality which recognized equal educational *outcome*, as well as access, had to wait rather longer – until the rise of the women's movement and the advent of a racially mixed society (Rubinstein, 1984).

In particular research evidence suggested that female pupils (and teachers) were at best undervalued and underrepresented in the work of schools, and at worst, ignored or harrassed (Spender, 1980: Kelly 1981: NUT 1980). So the gap between educational practice and the rhetoric of equality became more visible.

This prompted a flurry of publications from the DES and EOC describing the extent of sex differentiation and stereotyping in schools and its pedagogic and administrative implications (DES 1975, 1979, 1980, 1981; EOC – see appendix). In the main there was little analysis of why there were so few women and girls in key subject areas, top jobs or well paid industrial employment, although several academic research studies had indicated possible causal factors (Fogarty, 1971; Rapoport & Rapoport, 1978). The emphasis was placed firmly on the improvement of teaching methods and the careful dissemination of research findings for the benefit of *all* pupils, but with particular emphasis on the educational improvement of girls.

The suggestion that sex inequality in education was directly related to the general subordination of women by men, was largely ignored. Equality of opportunity, in this instance, was defined in terms of the current equal allocation of school resources and educational benefits rather than in any deliberate attempt at positive discrimination in favour of girls, to make up for past discriminatory experiences. In striving for equality within school, it was argued, boys would benefit as much as girls. In the same way that girls were to be encouraged to move into male dominated areas of the curriculum eg. science and technology, boys would be encouraged to take up traditionally female subjects such as the Arts and Humanities, and would accordingly be helped to become more sensitive and caring (Schools Council/ILEA, 1983).

Hence, when local authority money and resources became available, these tended to be awarded to those people who shared this view and who identified the following strategies for educational change:

Persuading girls to go into science and technology,

Providing a compulsory common core of subjects throughout schooling so that girls would be unable to drop the 'hard' sciences and boys would be compelled to take courses in child development or the Humanities,

Analysing textbooks, readers and classroom resources for stereoyping,

Reviewing aspects of school organization eg. registers, assemblies, uniform, disciplinary methods,

Devising non-sexist courses and materials aimed at changing the stereotyped perceptions of girls and boys,[6]

Encouraging discussion by running staff conferences and courses, and producing policy guidelines on equal opportunities,

Establishing mixed-sex, equal opportunities working parties (though usually dominated numerically by women) to develop and monitor school policy,

Creating posts of responsibility for equal opportunities – at inspectorate/advisor and at school level,

Establishing single-sex grouping in certain subjects ie. science, maths, to encourage girls to achieve the standards set by boys.

The principal aim of this equal opportunities approach was to encourage girls and women to move into privileged and senior positions in existing educational institutions rather than to seek any fundamental changes in schooling. Whilst it has been successful in getting issues of gender discussed widely and has been responsible for considerable change within school (eg. changes in the blocking of options at 13+ so that pupils are able to choose from non-traditional as well as traditional subjects, and more girls taking up science) it has, many feminists believe, made little impact on everyday school life and none at all on power and decision-making in education. Despite the increased discussion and activity in this area, many men (and some women) continue to remain indifferent or even hostile to the changes taking place or being suggested or promoted. Moreover decisions about whether girls and women should be given greater access to educational resources are still, in the main, taken by men and there has been little improvement in the appointment of women to senior educational posts. In fact, since the decline of single-sex schooling to make way for mixed comprehensives, the total number of female heads has actually declined (NUT, 1980; TES, 1983b).

Anti-sexist approaches to schooling; girl-centred education

> What does a woman need to know? Does she not, as a self-conscious self-defining human being, need a knowledge of her own history, her much politicised biology, an awareness of the creative work of women of the past, the skills and crafts and techniques and powers exercised by women in different times and cultures, a knowledge of women's rebellions and organised movements against our oppression and how they have been routed or diminished. Without such knowledge women live and have lived without a context, vulnerable to the projections of male fantasy, male prescriptions for us, estranged from our own experience because our education has not reflected or echoed it. I would suggest that not biology, but ignorance of ourselves, has been the key to our powerlessness.
>
> (Rich A., 'Taking Women's Studies Seriously' in
> *On Lies, Secrets & Silence*, 1980, p. 240)

Adrienne Rich argues that the ignorance of women about themselves and their culture has done much to confirm them in their oppressed state (see also Marina Foster's chapter); and that female education will need to undergo massive change before women overcome their subordination. She further identifies the (male) establishment and its power structure as the principal oppressor of girls and women.

Here lies the major difference between the egalitarians (those advocating equal opportunities) and the feminists (those advocating anti-sexist or girl-centred education).[7] Whereas the former fail to address the relationship between patriarchy, power and women's subordination, the latter place it at the centre of their thinking. They have expressed doubts about the value of policies of equal opportunities which deny or ignore competing educational (and economic) interests, and have criticized policies of educational change which fail to acknowledge the constant competition for power and control; between men and women, black people and white, and between class interests.

In this view, expanding educational opportunity is not just a question of juggling resources or rearranging option choices. It is far more fundamental than that. Feminists have recognized that if girls and women are to capture a greater slice of the educational 'cake', boys and men will have to give up their hold on the system – something they are unlikely to do without a struggle. Alternatively the egalitarians have made light of such issues as the politics of power and status and have tended to deal with immediate problems of school reform.

Whilst feminist teachers and parents have acknow-ledged the value of what has been achieved in the name of equal opportunities, they believe that the fight needs to carried further. To liberalize access to an inadequate sys-tem might be acceptable in the short term but for more per-manent change a major restructuring of all social institu-tions, including schools, is needed.

Their major concern in challenging sexism and discrimi-nation in schooling has been to place girls and women at the centre rather than at the periphery of the classroom and so challenge the dominance of male experience (Beecham 1983). They have used some of the same strategies as the egalitarians but their work in schools has also been based on some or all of the following premises:

Feminist education means girl or woman-centred educa-tion.

It has to take into account the actual (not stereotyped) experiences and lives of women and girls.

A curriculum needs to be provided which draws on the past and present experiences of women and girls.

Schooling, at the least, should furnish girls and young

women with the skills and knowledge to take on the male system 'out there', in the workplace.

Education should give girls and women a sense of solidarity with other members of their sex and hence a female-based confidence and motivation.

Certain characteristics of present day schooling such as hierarchical school organization, competitiveness, authoritarianism and selection should be replaced by new procedures based on cooperation, democracy, egalitarianism and community.

Feminist teachers, parents and pupils should be aware of the widespread oppression of women by men, and therefore be prepared for the struggles and opposition they are likely to encounter.

Feminists have applauded and worked for many of the changes instigated by the proponents of equal opportunities but they have also challenged the basic structure and practice of schooling, arguing that since the curriculum is male dominated, whether or not it is taught by women, it will have to change radically if girls are to find their place within it, These changes will include:

recognizing the importance of girl-centred study. What is *her*story or girls'/women's science or technology, or girl/woman centred mathematics or literature? And how do they differ from traditional (male-centred) forms of study?

exploring the relationship between sexuality, women's oppression and sexual harassment both at school and in the workplace,

developing girl-centred school organization so that girls

have the freedom, space, time and help to enable them genuinely to reach their full potential,[8]

providing wider horizons for girls to aim at, and, at the same time, not denigrate the lives and work of their mothers, friends and the women in their community,

establishing school girls' and women's groups to provide support for female pupils and members of staff.

Many of the contributors to this book have tried to work within the feminist framework but have nevertheless acknowledged and appreciated the equal opportunities initiatives which have enabled them to establish a broader base of support and understanding for their work.

Despite apparent consensus about equality of opportunity in our education system we have, in fact, a system designed to allocate success to the male, middle-class, white, able-bodied minority. Consequently people outside that privileged group, though they form the majority, are seen as somehow deficient. Policies of equal opportunities, in the past, have attempted to resolve this situation by trying to 'educate' girls, ethnic minorities, working-class and handicapped pupils to fit the white, middle-class, able bodied, male model. If, as is predictable the 'fit' is faulty, blame has been put on individual pupils rather than on the inadequacy of their schooling. The development of girl-centred education, the focus of this book, is an attempt to remove at least some of these structural injustices.

Notes

1. The EOC has dealt with a number of complaints by approaching the offending individual or institution on an informal basis, with the information that the law is being broken. In some instances, education authorities have changed their policies voluntarily eg. Somerset, 1982.

2. Girls have always had to gain a higher score at 11+ to go to grammar school so that the sex ratio of pupils is kept equal. If the same pass rates were applied to both sexes, about a third more girls than boys would have qualified for selective places.
3. It can be argued that those who subscribe to the ideology and policies of the present government were never interested in equality issues, and that Thatcherism holds to the rhetoric of equality *because* the legislation exists and only because of that.
4. For further research on sex differentiation in schooling see the appendix and bibliography.
5. An informative guide to the educational implications of the Sex Discrimination Act can be found in the EOC publication, *Do You Provide Equal Educational Opportunities?*, available free, on request (address in the appendix).
6. Curiously the most successful developments of non-sexist courses have been directed towards boys – namely the *Skills for Living* course at Hackney Downs School in ILEA, and the pack of materials produced by the convenors of the 1982 ILEA/ Schools Council conference, *Equal Opportunities; What's in it for boys?*
7. In this instance I have used the word feminist to describe a particular educational viewpoint. I do not wish to suggest, however, that equal opportunities and feminism are incompatible in general terms.
8. It may well be argued that single-sex schools now and in the past *have* provided girl-centred education which, nevertheless, has had little impact on the social position of women. However, many of the girls' schools in the state sector were grammar schools whose curricular, examinations and school organization were all designed to integrate into the national system which was, and is, male dominated.

CHAPTER 2

Structural Racism or Cultural Difference: Schooling for Asian girls

AVTAR BRAH & REHANA MINHAS

This chapter arises from our experiences as Asian women teachers/researchers in schools in West Yorkshire and London over the last seven years. We aim to highlight areas of concern for teachers rather than present a definitive theoretical analysis.

We start from the position that any discussion of Asian girls in British schools must be understood in the context of the complex social and historical processes which account for the subordination of black groups in British society. Social relations between white and black groups in Britain today are set against a background of colonialism and imperialism. Migration of black people to fill the labour shortages which followed the economic boom of the post-war years was largely a consequence of the economic exploitation and the subsequent 'underdevelopment' of the British colonies during the colonial period. The ideology of racism and its manifestations which sustained the colonial relationship have since undergone some important transformations in parallel with economic, political and ideological changes.

Since the Second World War racism in Britain has

increasingly become institutionalized (Minhas R., 1982). Contemporary racism now needs to be seen as a structural feature of the social system rather than a phenomenon merely of individual prejudice. The experience of Asian girls in schools is thus centrally shaped by the various manifestations of this new racism.

The experiences of Asian girls is also inscribed by their position as female in British society. As such they are subject to the sexual divisions prevailing in Britain but, unlike whites, they experience this oppression through the filter of racism. Asian girl's lives are also affected by the type of gender relations which exist amongst the particular Asian groups to which they belong. It is worth stressing that Asian girls are not a homogeneous category. They are identifiable, for instance, by religion, sect within a religion, linguistic group, caste and by the country from which their families originate. Each of these factors makes for a unique and distinctive experience; but the racist stereotypes that abound shift attention away from the need to understand the complexity of this experience.

In our view the position of Asians within the class structure of Britain is also central to an understanding of the life chances of Asian girls. The location of Asian labour within the lowest rungs of class hierarchy in Britain has had important consequences in all areas of social life, for instance, in the settlement patterns of Asian communities; in the type of schooling Asian children receive in inner city schools; and in the kind of labour Asian girls and boys are expected to perform in the present phase of the re-structuring of the British economy. The future trajectory of Asian girls' lives will owe a great deal to the class position of their families.

We wish to argue that our understanding of the position of Asian schoolgirls will remain limited, indeed distorted, unless we begin to identify how, why, and in what ways racism, gender and class inequalities are produced and reproduced within the education system and in society at large. We do not wish to imply that there is a simple one-to-one relationship between these three dimensions of an Asian girl's subordination with each oppression superimposed one on top of the other. Like Mary Fuller we would argue against such an 'additive model' (Fuller, 1983). We believe that the structures which reproduce racism, gender and class relations can have both complementary and contradictory effects.

Discussions about Asian girls rarely start from a structural perspective which takes into account the broader social context (recent exceptions include Parmar, 1982). By contrast they tend to utilize the twin notions of 'cultural clash' and 'inter-generational conflict' to explain away the problems that Asian girls may encounter as they pass through the education system. Young Asian girls growing up in Britain are thought to be exposed to two conflicting cultures, one at home and the other at school, as a consequence of which they are seen to experience stress and 'identity crisis'.

According to this view Asian girls internalize the supposedly superior Western values which conflict with the 'traditional' (and by implication inferior) customs and beliefs of their parents. In this ideological construction of Asian family life the two generations are presented as warring against each other with the adult generally depicted as authoritarian, uncompromising and oppressive.

By a simple sleight of hand these explanations dismiss the reality of racism, sexism and class inequality in shaping the life chances of Asian girls. Instead, the Asian family is constructed as the source of the problem. At the same time British society is presented as a homogeneous cultural entity devoid of conflict when, in fact, it encompasses a variety of class, regional and national cultures which complement or confront one another within the broader framework of power structures of Britain (Brah, 1982).

The pathologizing of the black family ie. presenting it, rather than structural inequality as the source of the problem, has parallels with the historical representation of the white working-class cultures as 'cultures of deprivation'. This, to us, is a key element in contemporary racism (John, 1981, CCCS, 1982).

Contrary to these popular stereotypes the majority of Asian girls have strong, positive and mutually supportive relationships with their parents. In a comparative study of Asian and white young people and their parents there was no evidence to show that the level of 'inter-generational conflict' among Asian families was any higher than amongst white families (Brah, 1979). Moreover, conflictual situations between parents and children, when they did arise, could, in the case of both Asian and white groups, be attributed to a variety of factors.

The 'cultural clash' explanation was found to have little value in understanding such conflict. Asian and white girls alike were found to experience aspects of family life as oppressive but there was no basis to infer that Asian girls were 'more oppressed' than white girls (Brah, op. cit.).

The *Times Educational Supplement* of 10.2.84 (Wilce) carries an article on Asian girls which epitomizes one of the ways in which ideologies about Asian girls are produced and reproduced. We feel it is important to draw attention to this article because appearing as it does in TES, it addresses a large educational audience and provides a clear illustration of how stereotypical images of Asian girls continue to persist and be reinforced in the education system.

From the outset the title, 'Walking the Tight-Rope Between Two Cultures' locates the parameters of the debate firmly within a cultural framework and shifts attention away from structural issues and concerns. The article begins with the sentence 'An Asian schoolgirl in Coventry turned to her teacher in despair because, she said, her father was beating her badly' and in so doing immediately invokes the racist image of the archetypal brutal and domineering Asian father. Irrespective of the actual intentions of the author the Asian family is by now already identified as the primary source of Asian girls' problems. In the classic 'between two cultures' and 'identity crisis' mode of explanations the article speaks of 'tensions of adolescence stretched to breaking point by the differing expectations of home, school and themselves'. No account is taken of the growing body of literature which challenges the very concept of 'normal tensions of adolescence' as a universal phenomenon. The ideological assertion of most things Western as superior to Eastern is achieved through expressions of pity for the girls arriving home from school and 'changing from school uniform to Shalwar Kameez (the traditional dress of the Punjab), from English to Punjabi, and from noisy self-expression to a more subdued form of behaviour' (TES, op. cit.). It is clear to us that the author has no intimate knowledge about the private sphere of Punjabi family life and its dynamic and vibrant Punjabi female cultures. Moreover, who is to decide whether the Western mode of dress is superior to Shalmar Kameez, or English to Punjabi?

In a subsequent paragraph the author speaks of the 'narrow groove' of an Asian girl's life which she sees as 'strictly bounded by religious and family gatherings, the television and the video'. This leads us to raise the question: How exciting a life does a white working-class girl lead? What opportunities does she have to supposedly widen her horizons through activities prescribed as 'valuable by the middle class'? We would ask the headmistress of a Bradford school quoted in the article as saying 'And what do you do when it comes to English 'O' level exams and the subject is "A Walk in the Country?" ', how many white working-class children from inner-city areas are in the habit of pursuing country walks as a favourite past-time? Do the material circumstances of working-class families have nothing to do with the kind of leisure activities they can afford? It is ironic that a remark such as the above is made about a community which actually has rural origins!

Of course, in the interest of 'good journalistic balance' the author of this article quotes two Asian community workers and a white equal-opportunities adviser from a London LEA, all of whom stress the danger of reinforcing stereotypes of Asian girls by highlighting extreme cases. But their comments are reported in the second half of the article by which time the main agenda has already been set, a range of stereotypes confirmed, and alternative, oppositional ideas rendered effectively marginal.

We believe the above article encapsulates many of the current ideologies about Asian girls which influence teachers' orientations towards them. We challenge the notion that schools are 'politically neutral institutions' and that the professional 'code of conduct' stops teachers' personal beliefs from affecting their pedagogical practices and their day-to-day relationships with pupils. As Stuart Hall (1978, p. 166) argues with reference to 'practical ideologies of racism'; when people construct explanations they imagine that they are doing so free from ideological and societal constraints – but in fact all explanations are the product of ideologies constructed over a period of time.

Educational institutions are a microcosm of society, playing their part in the production and reproduction of inequalities. (Note, we are not suggesting that schools are the 'perfect mechanisms of cultural reproduction' as that would deny the dynamics of resistance and over-simplify a complex process (CCCS, 1982: Jessop, 1982)). Hence a frequent comment made by teachers, perhaps to stress the 'political neutrality of the schools' and their 'professionalism' is that: 'there is no racism here, I treat all the children the same, black or whatever colour'. This particular approach of denying pupils their racial/cultural identities is just one way in which racism is made manifest.

Another common experience of Asian girls in school is that they are labelled 'passive' or 'docile'. In classroom practice this has often meant that the girls are systematically forgotten or ignored when it comes to demands on the teachers' time, except when the perennial topics of 'arranged marriages' and 'polygamy' are discussed. In one extreme case a teacher stated that 'she could not tell one Asian girl from another in her class . . . and that it didn't matter, so long as they were quiet'. It is therefore hardly surprising that a popular comment which appears on the school reports of Asian girls is 'she rarely participates in class discussion . . . shy, quiet, lacking in self-confidence but well behaved'. In our experience when Asian girls do challenge this stereotype of being 'passive', they are dealt with more severely than their counterparts.

The other dominant stereotypes which prevail in school about Asian girls lead to the categorization of the girls as either the 'exotic oriental mystics' or as the rejects – 'ugly', 'smelly', 'oily-haired', 'wearing baggy trousers' or 'Pakis'. Often Asian girls who are categorized as 'sexual rejects' are subjected to a great deal of verbal abuse. Many Asian girls have their names mis-pronounced, or are given derogatory nick-names or are even called by an English name.

Further ridicule is experienced by Asian girls who wish to wear the Shalwar Kameez in schools which have a strict school uniform policy. Thus their only option is to wear trousers underneath the school skirt.

The sexual and racial harassment of Asian girls in co-educational situations is condoned for the most part, because such harassment is often attributed to the Asian girls' 'inability to stand up for themselves'. In one particular incident when a case of sexual/racial harassment was reported to a teacher she said: 'Well we can't shelter them, surely they will face similar situations out of school, they might as well learn to cope with them . . .' (the girls had been sexually molested by a group of boys). In the same school great 'concern' was expressed because the Asian girls went round in a 'gang' during break times, congregated in the library during the lunch break and according to some staff 'made no effort to integrate'! Needless to say the girls' attempts to organize and protect one another were not recognized and were in fact seen as a reflection of their 'in-balanced personalities and sheltered existence'. We also know of incidents where Asian girls have to protect themselves against physical attacks.

In our experiences when the issue of sexism is raised in relation to Asian school girls, it is immediatiately perceived as 'a cultural dilemma', 'the oppression brought about by arranged marriages' or the 'macho-chauvinism of Asian men', rather than the experience of sexism and racism in schools, in society or in the labour market. In the context of such discussions, schools are divorced from society at large and are seen as 'those liberating institutions' which give Asian girls space to compare their archaic cultures with those of 'the enlightened West'. Thus the focus is on the 'demerits of Asian culture' rather than the processes at work in education which reinforce inequalities, through the formal and hidden curriculum.

The racism and sexism experienced by Asian schoolgirls *vis-à-vis* careers counselling has been well documented by Pratibha Parmar and Nadira Mirza (1983) in their article 'Stepping Forward . . . Work with Asian Young Women'. For instance Asian girls are often discouraged from pursuing more academic careers with the cautionary advice that their 'aspirations are too high, unrealistic', and that they are 'probably going to be married off anyway, so don't waste time . . .'. Contrary to the popular stereotype which suggests that all Asian parents are opposed to further education for their daughters, in our experience there is tremendous parental support for higher education for girls even in non-conventional careers such as engineering and sciences. Statistics compiled recently by the NUS which focus on Asian parents who object to further education for their daughters, do not mention the substantial number of Asian parents who support higher education for their daughters. We do not deny, however, that some Asian parents do object to further education for their daughters as indeed do some white working-class parents.

A further aspect of school racism and sexism centres on the organization of the curriculum. Those Asian schoolgirls who are identified as 'English as a Second Language Learners' (ESL) often have access only to a restricted curriculum. The criteria used to 'identify pupils with language difficulties' are haphazard just as the quality of ESL provision varies greatly from school to school. The 'ESL' label is at times synonymous with 'remedial' thus further restricting fourth- and fifth-year option choices in Secondary Schools. Often the ESL girls find themselves channelled to do a range of 'practical subjects' such as Childcare, Needlecraft, Home Economics, Communication Skills, Everyday Maths and if 'lucky', Office Practice.

We are not criticizing these practical subjects, but question the 'reasoning' which subjects the ESL girls to a restricted curriculum. The offer of a restricted curriculum is part and parcel of the institutional processes which undermine the educational chances for Asian girls and have serious implications for the labour market.

Non-ESL Asian schoolgirls are also subjected to the selection processes in school which channel them to particular options, subjects, sets, 'CSE/'O' levels. The Asian schoolgirls whom we interviewed felt that subject teachers often did not fully explain the merits or otherwise of taking certain subject combinations *vis-à-vis* the girls' intended careers. Within the sciences, physics was considered to be 'suitable' only for a small number of girls. The girls said that they were often not given the benefit of a second chance after mock examinations. Additionally they felt strongly that the objections raised by white pupils and their parents about school decisions relating to public examinations, were taken far more seriously than those of Asians. We consider that the whole process of counselling pupils for option choices and the channelling of girls into certain subjects needs to be examined critically and researched further.

While we do not suggest that changes in the formal and hidden curriculum will automatically lead to radical changes in the structure of society at large, we would argue that teachers and other educationalists need to critically review their pedagogical practices and make a firm commitment to challenging sexist and racist practices in their institutions. Of course there are teachers committed to anti-racist/anti-sexist teaching whose efforts need to be encouraged and acknowledged. Nevertheless we contend that the content of the curriculum in British schools is in the main Euro-centric, explicitly and implicitly racist, sexist and biased against the working class.

Though racism and sexism are distinct phenomenas with different histories, teachers should not fall into the trap of 'choosing' between them (Taylor, 1984). The experience of black women can only be adequately understood from a perspective which recognizes that black women are subject to the simultaneous oppression of race, sex, and class. Sadly we have come across white feminist teachers who argue that because the relationship between gender and race is so complex they have chosen not to address the issue of racism.

It is our belief that when teachers address only sexism as problematic the experience of black schoolgirls is rendered 'invisible'. This also implies that the experience of black women is similar to that of white women, ignoring the fact that white women stand in a power relation as oppressors of black women.

Moreover there is a tendency for some feminist and other teachers to adopt the pathological model of the Asian family only too readily, without acknowledging the support the family network gives to its members in the context of British society, and without understanding values/cultures which are not European. For instance, the acceptance of the 'pathological authoritarian family model' is illustrated through the selection of teaching material such as 'Parveen' by Anne Mehdevi (Penguin/Peacock publications).

'Parveen' is about the experiences of a 16 year old who goes to stay with her father in Persia – her father invites her to judge the case of a woman beaten to blindness and subsequently rejected by both her husband and her brother for refusing to serve her husband's second wife and her two sons. The story of Parveen, especially the extract of the court session (pp. 51–59) is considered to be an excellent entrée to the topic of Woman's Aid. Very rarely are extracts chosen which illustrate the struggles of Asian women against colonialism or current struggles against state racism eg. fighting the immigration laws, or Asian women's struggles to gain trade union recognition? By choosing to ignore the campaigns of Asian women, and the Asian schoolgirl's experience of inequality, the continual focus on the perennial topics, 'arranged marriages', 'the brutality of Islamic laws' reinforce the prevailing racist and sexist myths of Asian families and Asian females – in particular the myth of the 'passive' female.

In the schools that we worked in, we observed that groups of Asian girls were aware of the stereotypes which prevailed and resisted them in a variety of ways. For example, as a reaction against the notion that all Asian pupils have language difficulties, a group of Asian girls insisted on speaking in Urdu in the class. They deliberately ignored the demands made by the subject teachers, stating that they had not understood the instructions. In another case the teacher's ignorance of Punjabi culture was played upon by the girls, who tried to resist school rules by insisting (incorrectly) that the wearing of jewellery was an important part of their religion and culture. In our opinion the most organized form of resistance is the increasing number of Asian girls' groups being formed under their own initiative. These groups give solidarity and support to their members and spaces for Asian girls to exchange experiences and challenge the school structures which oppress them.

School policy should include a serious and continuous review of both institutional practices such as assessment, examinations, reports, selection processes and forms of punishment, and at classroom level, pedagogy and resources.

In conclusion we would like to briefly look at the question of strategies for action to combat racism and sexism in education. Of course, this is a complex issue; and there are no simple and straightforward 'blue-prints'. In our view it is important that school practice is informed by an understanding of the broader social context within which racism and sexism are embedded. We need to make connections between what goes on in schools and what happens in society as a whole.

As teachers, we need to examine critically the structure, organization and operations of both the LEA and the schools in which we teach. We should also develop an anti-racist and anti-sexist curriculum in schools. As distinct from the formal curriculum, we also need to look critically at the kind of ethos sustained in school through its 'hidden curriculum'. It is equally important to challenge the racism/sexism of teachers and pupils.

Finally we believe that teachers and other educationalists need to break away from a narrow Euro-centric mode of thinking and teaching which contributes to the devaluation of black cultures and experiences. For it is only by recognizing the value of cultures and experiences other than their own and by working together to develop and refine anti-racist and anti-sexist practice that teachers can genuinely begin to think about education and equality as compatible notions.

CHAPTER 3

Sexual Tyranny: Male violence in a mixed secondary school

CAROL JONES

Introduction

In this chapter I aim to give a brief overview of my research into male violence in one secondary school; to then question the safety of mixed sex schooling for girls[1] and to suggest ways of challenging male violence in schools.

Research on sexual harassment was carried out over a nine-month period, in 1982, in a mixed Comprehensive School on the outskirts of London; and took the form of my own observations as well as interviews[2] with pupils, ancilliary workers and teachers at the school. For the purpose of this chapter I have focused on what happened to girls at the school on the basis that girls' experience is seen to be even less credible than adult women's – their experiences are often not validated or documented – and as such they have had to remain publicly silent. Women teachers and some girls have written of their experience of sexual harassment elsewhere (Whitbread, A. 1980; Spare Rib, June 1983).

Motivation to do this research was based on my own experience as a teacher in various mixed-sex schools and as a feminist campaigning against male violence. It disturbed me that so many girls and women I knew, in different schools, were being subjected to daily sexual harassment from boys and men. Yet as with all forms of male violence there seemed to be a public silence surrounding the issue. My aim was to break that silence.

Sexual tyranny in one school

The Message on the Wall

Feminists have documented the content and messages of pornography which range from 'page three' photos and men's magazines to 'snuff' movies in which women are actually tortured and eventually murdered (Barry 1981; Dworkin 1981; Lederer 1980; W.A.V.A.W. June 1982).

The central themes of domination, control, humiliation and mutilation of women by men serve as propaganda by which men learn that it is acceptable to abuse women and girls. This propaganda was evident at the school in the form of 'woman-hating' graffiti ('Miss Smith is a pro' and 'Sharon is a slag') and even pornography.

Hanging in the main foyer was a large oil painting of a dismembered woman's body, with stilettos and darts in the background. The image was a violent one, depicting women as submissive and passive objects to be violated. It had been painted by a boy at the school. Although women and girls at the school had campaigned to have the painting removed, male teachers, who were overwhelmingly in positions of authority within the school, united to defend the painting as 'art' and belittled the women's complaints.

There were other examples of pornography and sexual imagery in the school, not always under the guise of art. Boys drew erect penises on many available surfaces. One teacher reported that a 'Girls Are Powerful' poster – which had been put up to give girls support in her mixed classroom – had been destroyed by boys who'd written 'we're here to stay' and drawn erect penises on it.

The boys were clearly responding to the girls' growing confidence by asserting symbols of their sexuality, their power.

Magazine cutouts and pictures of women (often put up to brighten the building!) were generally covered by drawings of erect penises entering any available orifice – women's mouths, ears, between their legs.

Perhaps the most disturbing imagery was in the boys' accounts of the violent videos they'd watched at home. Many teachers are now familiar with the way in which pupils swop descriptions of 'video nasties', taking pleasure in graphically describing to each other the mutilation of women.

Those who can stomach the videos become heroes among their friends, swopping videos and visiting each others' homes to watch women being cut up on the screen. It seems that girls are also being judged by their 'ability' to watch these horrors although most girls I have spoken to were disturbed by their contents, though often afraid to say so publicly. It appears that young people are being anaesthetised into an acceptance of the butchering of women.

Girls at the school also complained that boys teased them with pornography. 'Michael used to bring in "Playboy" and hold it up to Sharon 'cos she's shy and say, "Hey!, you got one of these?" ' One woman teacher discovered a boy masturbating in a classroom to a photograph of a naked woman. He ejaculated to the cheers of other boys.

Sexual harassment

In most schools verbal sexual harassment is an everyday experience for girls and women teachers. Every girl I spoke to gave the same list of words used against them – 'cunts', 'slag', 'pro', 'bitch'.

As girls walked into the class groups of boys jeered, commented on the size of girls' breasts and on their appearance. Almost all the comments were sexual, although black girls also had racist abuse levelled against them. Black girls frequently expressed their anger. 'We have a harder time here', said one of them, the boys are all loud-mouths.' Male teachers, too, subjected both girls and women teachers to suggestive sexual comments, appraising looks and leers. The men often referred to girls in a sexual way in the staff-room and made jokes about the girls' bodies.

Direct sexual harassment and assaults were common. Girls complained, 'You see them (boys) touching girls up all the time in the corridors and that.' Some girls had been seriously assaulted, 'They (a group of boys) pushed me and I was punched. I've got scars, look! From their fags. They burned me . . . Mr —— had a word with them but that was all.' The reason for this treatment – 'I used to complain about them, about the way they are to us. I wouldn't laugh at their stupid jokes.' Another girl confirmed, 'Of course they touch us up all the time: they're boys', One girl talked of her fear of walking home from school after being sexually assaulted by two boys at school. She found it too upsetting to describe what they'd done to her. A woman teacher spoke of an incident in her class, 'Darren was going out with Tracy in the same class. He sat next to her and kept punching her. As soon as I told her to move away from him, he said, "shut up or you'll get the same as her!"'

Male teachers were quite open about their attitudes towards the girls, often putting their arms around the girls, and making comments such as, 'You're looking gorgeous today.' Girls talked of being sexually assaulted by male teachers, 'I didn't really want to go to see Mr —— but he said, "Put your chair here love" and he kept reaching over me. I didn't know what to do.'

Another girl reported, 'Mr —— stopped me in the corridor and asked me if I had a school book then tried to get me in the stock room. He said I was well developed.' 'Mr —— used to go out with this girl at school but every-one was talking about it. He kept phoning her up.' Women teachers reported that some of the girls had come to them complaining of a couple of male teachers whom the girls described as 'funny' and 'perverted'.

Sexual Abuse Outside of School

The sexual violence that girls were experiencing from boys and men at school was, for many of them, additional to sexual assaults at home from fathers, brothers, uncles, grandfathers. It is well known that sexual assault of girls in the family is common but nevertheless is rarely discussed (Jeffreys, 1982a; Nelson, S., 1982; Rush, F., 1980; Ward, E., 1984)[4]

In this school, girls occasionally confided in women teachers who were themselves unsure of how to react, particularly if it threw up memories of the teachers' past experience of being abused, or if they had experienced battering and rape in their marriages. Women teachers at the school were conscious that some girls were being sexually abused by their brothers, whom the women also taught.

Reactions, Rebellion, Resistance at School

It was apparent that male violence – visual, verbal and physical sexual harassment – was part of daily school life. But it would be a mistake to assume that the girls and women were passive victims.

Girls'/Women's strategies for dealing with harassment depended on the length of time they'd been at the school. The longer the woman had been teaching, or the older the girl, the less likely she was to report cases of assault, knowing that she was unlikely to be believed or that boys were inadequately punished. Sexual harassment was not recognized as a problem because the men did not experience it. As such, sexual harassment did not, apparently, 'exist'. Knowing this, women/girls did not report cases. Because so few incidents were reported, the men in positions of authority were able to argue that sexual harassment was not a problem in school.

Girls were adamant about 'fighting back' and often supported each other when attacks on them occurred. For this they were severely punished by both the hierarchy and the boys. For instance, a second-year girl had been suspended for going to a first-year girls' assistance when the girl was being assaulted by a boy. The boy remained at school.

Another girl was found with her fists clenched, crying, in the girls' toilet by a woman teacher who said,

> she had been assaulted by the same boy for a number of weeks . . . she was staring into the mirror saying, 'I hate them, I hate them'. We talked about other ways of dealing with it. Nothing else was done – well, she was suspended for throwing a chair at the boy and he stayed on at the school.

The entire fourth-year girls were considered to be troublesome because they stood up for themselves and each other. They asked for a room to be set aside for them to go to at lunchtime. Women teachers were keen to support them but were accused of encouraging their rebellious behaviour.

At times girls and women teachers defended each other – a teacher said,

> it was ridiculous, the boy who'd pulled Michelle's blazer off was pulling her one way and two girls and I were pulling him off. I thought, that sums it up: we have to protect each other now.

Male teachers claimed not to have come across many cases of sexual harassment in their classes. When they gave examples of any conflict they described them as 'discipline problems'. Boys, however, were quite open about their feelings towards girls in the school, 'I hate them, they're all slags' said one. Another admitted that boys used force if girls confronted them although he felt so powerful that he ignored the girls' resistance to him, 'I don't give a shit if the girls are rude to me . . . well, I just ignore them, they're all slags anyway.'

Rebellion broke out, finally, in a staff meeting called to discuss 'discipline problems' in the school. One feminist teacher raised the issue of sexual harassment arguing that it must be central to discussions on 'discipline'. She spoke of the harassment as experienced by girls from boys, by women from boys and by all girls/women from male staff. All the men – including normally 'sympathetic' men – became defensive and aggressive claiming that she was exaggerating. At this point individual women stood up and gave lists of examples in which girls as well as themselves were daily subjected to assaults from men/boys: 'The girls have a bloody awful time here. They've got to be tough to survive.' said one. Another, 'parents should know what's happening to their daughters – it's terrible for girls at school.'

Arguments broke out in which racist 'explanations' were given for 'problems' in the school – that boys from ethnic minority groups had a low opinion of women. Apart from the fact that these attacks were unfounded and perpetuate cultural myths and stereotypes, they ignore the fact that violence came from all the boys and adult men regardless of ethnic or cultural background.

This was the first time that the issue of male violence had been openly raised in the school. The response was total polarization between the staff along sex lines. The women had, until that time, been fairly isolated from each other, and had not realized that in fact every one of them had witnessed daily sexual harassment towards girls and women in the school.

The staff meeting affected the course of action immediately. Women who had previously not had a great deal in common with each other started talking more openly together and formed a women's group. Information about the staff meeting was passed on to some of the girls who, in turn, talked with other girls about strategies against male violence in the school.

Boys and male teachers responded by punishing the women more directly (increasing their sexual attacks) and attempted to humiliate individual women in front of each other by jeering and laughing when women walked down the corridors. They also refused to talk to some of the feminists.

The hierarchy, wishing to make it appear that assaults were being taken more seriously, publicly announced every occasion a boy was reprimanded. This 'reprimand' usually amounted to warnings such as (as one year head told me), 'I could go to prison for what you've done lad. If it could happen to me it could happen to you.' Boys responded by defending and protecting their space even more and became more abusive, particularly to the feminist teachers whom they presumably blamed for the girls' resistance to them.

Explanations

Schools do not exist in a social vacuum. They reflect and reproduce the power relations within a male supremacist society – a society in which the dominant group (men) ultimately maintain their power position through force. So, men/boys bring to school the values and experiences of a 'woman-hating' society, a society which promotes pornography and the expanding sex industry and belittles sexual violence in the family, i.e. sexual abuse of girls, rape, wife beating, as well as outside the family.

Men/boys who violate us are not unusual. They are 'normal' men: all classes, ages and races of men are capable of sexual violence. As such, men/boys at school are no different from the men who buy pornography, beat women, assault their daughters (and other girls) and abuse their sisters and mothers. We, as women, cannot afford to see boys as 'innocent children' or male teachers as sympathetic professionals. Men/boys who do not sexually harass women/girls benefit from those who do as it maintains their power position as a (sex) class.

Male violence in mixed schools serves to support boys as they practise their sexual domination over girls and it attempts to teach girls that it is 'natural' for them to be tyrannized by men into a subordinate position. Or, as one fourth-year girl commented, 'you learn how the boys treat you so it's given me more experience for when I leave!'

Despite the fact that the writings of many women, since the seventeenth century, have been rendered invisible and have had to be 'rediscovered' (Spender 1982b) we know that many First Wave Feminists[5] and some present day feminists have made connections between male violence and male sexual behaviour (Coveney *et al*, 1984); (Jeffreys, 1982b). They have argued that the political institution of heterosexuality is an area of struggle in which male domination and women's subordination can be most powerfully reinforced and maintained.

As such, heterosexuality, as a system to contain women, has been actively promoted at times when women have been stepping out of line (challenging male supremacy). This promotion of heterosexuality – to regulate women's behaviour – has come in different guises throughout this century beginning with the liberalizing of (hetero) sex through the Sex Reform Movement in the 1920s. (Jeffreys 1983) and the rise of the science of sexology to the growth in the 1960s of the 'permissive society'. For example, the (false) ideology of the 1960's sexually 'permissive society' was (hetero) sexual equality; a belief that free and available sex was a 'good thing' for women and that we should become as sexually 'active' as men. In practice this resulted in the affirmation and strengthening of male domination and the legitimation of male violence through the expanding pornography and sex industry. That ideology continues.

The 1960s 'sexual revolution' coincided with the promotion of a particular educational philosophy – the philosophy of mixed-sex education as developed by R. R. Dale; and was taken up by consecutive governments. Introducing mixed education was seen as a progressive move ultimately leading to equality between the sexes. However, it may well be true that mixed education serves unwittingly to strengthen male domination.

Moreover, we have been encouraged to believe that

mixed comprehensive education is the only progressive and egalitarian system of education: mixed comprehensives are better resourced than single-sex girls' comprehensives (Byrne, 1978), but that is hardly surprising given that women's education is so undervalued. It has sometimes been seen as regressive and prudish to challenge mixed education, in the same way as it has been considered prudish and 'right wing' to criticize male sexuality (particularly if that criticism extends to attacking men's pornography).[6]

Some of us are now convinced that mixed-sex schools are dangerous places for girls and women and that they exist to further benefit boys as they establish their sexual domination over girls. We should not be hoodwinked into subscribing to a system which is detrimental to girls in the name of 'progressive' education.

What Can Be Done

At present, given the economic and political climate, it is unlikely that educational policy will shift from mixed to single-sex schooling for girls. Nevertheless, there are things that can be done to challenge male violence in schools:

1. Anti-sexist initiatives in mixed Comprehensive Schools have included single-sex groupings for certain subjects, for example, The DASI Project in London (Cornbleet & Libovitch 1983), so that girls are able to develop an awareness and confidence together: be in a stronger position to support each other against the boys and create strategies for change.
2. Each school should set up women's groups for teachers, parents and ancilliary staff for mutual support, sharing of experiences and discussing action. Girls' groups should also be set up and both groups work together on strategies for dealing with sexual harassment. Possibilities include keeping an 'incident book' in which

girls/women record sexual assaults. This not only serves to validate girls'/women's experience but may also be useful as 'proof' should the school need convincing. Women/girls should take responsibility for dealing with sexual harassment, to show that women are a powerful force.

3. A room for girls to spend time together is essential so that they do not have to seek refuge in the girls' toilets (many girls do this because it is the only place that is theirs – boys take up the majority of space in the school).

   Men/boys are not likely to take well to these changes and may become abusive to womens/girls groups. Tact is, of course, very useful when under this kind of pressure.

4. Certain local education authorities are currently promoting 'Equal Opportunities' policies in an attempt to combat inequalities on grounds of sex and race. Some schools have therefore formed equal opportunities groups which differ from women-only groups in that they are often mixed.[7] Policies of equal opportunities appear to raise issues of sexual inequalities by focusing on improving 'equality' between girls and boys. This approach disguises the power relations between the sexes by failing to identify the problem of boys. In other words, altering images in books to provide positive role models for girls or teaching women's studies can make little difference to a girl's self esteem when she is being constantly harassed by boys and men at school.

   The implementation of an anti-sexist policy will identify the problem (boys/men) and attempt to address that issue as a key move to improving the school curriculum.

5. One of the most supportive things a school can do is for the women's/girls' group to keep in touch with outside feminist support groups and agencies, for example Rape Crisis; Incest Survivors' Campaign; Women's Aid and W.A.V.A.W.[8]

   The London Rape Crisis Centre runs a twenty-four hour counselling service for any woman or girl who has experienced any kind of male violence – including all kinds of sexual assault and rape.

When a girl confides in a woman teacher, apart from making sure the teacher believes her, does not break her confidence or try to take over, either the girl or the teacher may well phone a Rape Crisis Centre or contact the Incest Survivors' Campaign for further advice. If in any doubt, I recommend that women phone Rape Crisis.

6. As women, we all experience some form of male violence but we often feel alone, believing that we are in some way to blame. As such, women who are assaulted at home – whether as daughters, sisters, wives or mothers – may feel isolated.

   It may therefore well be of benefit for women at school to provide 'women only' tutor groups to organize courses on male violence as experienced by women, particularly in dealing with family issues.

7. Finally, if we all talk openly and often about male violence and become more concerned about it we may succeed in breaking the silence surrounding what is happening to girls in mixed schools.

Notes

1. I am using the term 'girls' here to include all girls and young women at the school. The term is used throughout this chapter to distinguish between (girl) pupils and (women) teachers. However, as I am specifically referring to girls in a secondary school, the term 'girls' usually refers to young women.

2. I used structured, open-ended, interview questions to (tape) record the experience of women and male teachers (who were selected to include teachers on scales one to four) and girls and boys of mixed abilities from each year group in the school. The sample included members of ethnic groups. Interviews were informal and supportive usually developing into conversations. I have changed the names of the school and individuals I spoke to in order to protect their identities.

3. One woman teacher sent me a 'story' written by a fourteen year old boy in her class which read like the script for a porn-ographic film. In the composition a feminist teacher's flat is broken into by the boy; she is assaulted, raped, hung up, butchered, her body cut up and thrown around the room. Upon leaving the flat, the boy declares, 'And now mother, your turn.' The teacher who sent the piece was deeply distressed. Her school was a mixed and predominantly middle-class school outside London. The boy who'd written the piece (who'd played the part of an anti-sexist man in a recent school play) did not understand why the teacher was angry.

4. This area of male violence is surrounded by public silence and many myths. It is beyond the scope of this chapter to expand on what is surely of crucial concern to women and girls, but I would refer girls/women to 'Sexual Violence' (London Rape Crisis Centre 1984, 87–109). Additionally, suggestions and support agencies are listed at the end of the book.

5. First Wave Feminism – the term used to describe the first women's movement – is generally regarded as the period from the mid nineteenth century to the first two decades of the twentieth century in Britain. The movement was global although 'First Wave' in India extended from the 1880s to the 1940s. (Sarah, 1982).

6. By focusing only on 'censorship', writers who wish to defend 'video nasties'/pornography seem to insist on aligning feminists who are critical of male violence on the screen with the increasingly alarming 'right wing' ideology of a Tory Britain. (Raynor, R., 1984(a+b) I see this as an attempt to silence women who are angry at the butchering of women yet who are also disturbed by the increasing power of the right. It needs to be made clear, here, that feminists campaigning against male violence do not share any political sympathies with the Mary Whitehouse campaign or 'moral majority' (in fact quite the opposite) but that does not mean that we must keep silent about the mutilation of women.

7. It has recently come to light that one such E.O. group took up the suggestion of keeping an incident book for cases of sexual assault. The men, who were in positions of authority in the school, threatened to take action against women teachers through the N.U.T. – presumably realizing that they could now easily be named for harassment in the incident book.

Much as it is pleasing to hear male teachers admitting so readily to harassment, it is disturbing that a Union that serves both women and men, may be used to limit women's strategies against male violence, and in so doing condone it.

8. The telephone numbers and Contact addresses are to be found in Appendix 2.

CHAPTER 4

A Curriculum for All? The Relationship between Racism, Feminism and Schooling: A personal view

MARINA FOSTER

Introduction

In October 1981 at a seminar held in the Royal Festival Hall, ILEA presented research evidence on the 'effect of social class, ethnic background and sex of pupils upon academic achievement in its schools', to teachers and representatives from all its educational institutions.

The research evidence presented in these reports gave rise to a great deal of concern about the educational future of the present generation of pupils in ILEA schools and colleges. It showed that in an apparently unbiased system, certain groups of children were not benefiting from their schooling, and what is more, they, rather than the education system, were being blamed for it.

Concern deepened with the publication of research such as that of Sally Tomlinson which revealed the extent of educational inequality. Tomlinson interviewed 25 black women and found the women's perceptions of the level of education they had achieved, very revealing. She reported that they considered themselves 'lucky' to have achieved university, both because of their race and their gender.

> I'm lucky to be at university, most of my school friends are doing secretarial courses, – the teachers didn't push them because they were black.

> At college you are really isolated if you are the only black women, and you usually are . . .

Evidence now available from other studies indicates a national trend rather than a specifically ILEA phenomenon. (Fuller, M. 1980, Tomlinson, S., 1983)

What can we do?

It is going to take more than a leap of the imagination to close the gap and to reinstate women and girls in an equal and fairer position *vis-à-vis* boys at all levels of education. A concentration on resources alone (i.e. books and pictures) will take generations to eradicate the effects of patriarchal attitudes and low expectations of girls, held by men and women teachers alike.

To ensure the right of each and every girl and boy to develop her or his full potential, detailed guidance will have to be provided to re-evaluate current practices and beliefs about sex differences. More importantly recognition needs to be given to those examples of sound pedagogical practices which in the long term will lead towards greater educational equality. However, before we will be able to achieve this, we will need to recognize the implications of the research mentioned earlier.

It has been argued that the nature of women's socialization guarantees our oppression and that schooling is an important part of that process of socialization (Mitchell, 1971). Moreover, one cannot but agree with Hooks when she maintains that though the slogans 'women are wonderful' and 'black is beautiful' are crucial elements in the rights movement, they offer only part of the picture: 'they must go hand in hand with a knowledge of what *our oppression has done to retard us'* (My emphasis Hooks, 1981).

A statement by black women at a conference of OWAAD (The Organization of Women of Asian and African descent) in March 1979 spelt this out:

> Education is not about allowing us to realise our full potential; it is not about encouraging us to exercise our minds to the full or creating self-aware individuals. Rather the education system seeks to grade and discipline the majority of school leavers for the world of work outside. With our understanding of the jobs black people do, it is obvious what kind of education we are going to get; we do the worse jobs in society and are well prepared for this by receiving the worse kind of education.

The OWAAD women highlight educational practices and beliefs in education which they see as militating against us and our struggle. Amongst these practices and beliefs are:

1 the existence of sexist bias in education;
2 the conspicuous absence of black women figures in learning materials, and
3 the stereotypes that exist of black women

> The only real concept that exists is the two-fold image held by society at large of big, 'black mammy' and 'exotic prostitute'. (op. cit. OWAAD, 1979).

In referring to teachers and the education system they further maintain:

> all too frequently they (teachers) refused to accept responsibility for the miseducation of black children. They prefer instead to blame parents, environment, upbringing or the effects of immigration . . . The cuts in spending on education have particularly affected schools in run-down working class areas – areas where the majority of black children are to be found. Those, we know, are the schools that already face difficulties such as lack of resources, a high teacher turnover, poor buildings, inadequate classrooms
> (op. cit. OWAAD, 1979).

How very apt are these observations in the present economic climate.

So, how do we counter the cycle of disadvantage experienced by our daughters; since women's struggle for freedom and justice has always been under threat one way or another.

One way must be to inspire and motivate girls by teaching them about the often forgotten struggles and achievement of women. For those reasons, women will need to re-write history to tell future generations '*her*-story', and already feminists, historiographers and researchers have done much to restore women to their rightful place in the search for social justice and equality.

Continuity or discontinuity

One important issue arises out of study of the black woman's part in the feminist demands for social justice and equality. This is the continuity/discontinuity between the women's struggle and the black women's struggle; that black and white women are joined in their oppression as women but are divided by their ethnicity. This was first identified by Constance Carroll, a member of the University of Pittsburgh's Advisory Council on Women's Opportunities, (Hull, *et al.*, 1982), who also described the 'tacit formulae followed by all black women who wish to succeed in a man's world'.

> You must be *better qualified* than the men.
> You must be more *articulate*.
> You must be more *aggressive*.
> You must have *more stamina* to face inevitable setbacks.
> You must have *more patience*, since you will advance *more slowly*.
> Above all, you must remain *feminine* and not appear threatening.

She continues –

> I have found that black women share these dicta with white women. However, black women have an extra step in the syllogism which white women do not have, that is, they must also be better than white women. It is this seldom discussed fact which has generated bitterness towards white women in general.

This is also the reason why many of us believe that black women must conduct their own struggle (Carby, 1982). On the power ladder, white women may be two steps removed from power, but black women are three steps removed. In an unequal system the black woman cannot help being cautious in allying herself with a 'privileged' competitor. Moreover, the treble handicap (black, women and working class) which black women face daily cannot but reflect back on our children. We have lost out so far in the competition that it often seems impossible for us to catch up. Do we black mothers now train our daughters to act on their own or do we leave it up to 'our white sisters, radical friends'? Of course this is a rhetorical question since mothers see the teaching of survival strategies, whatever these might be, in whatever culture, as an integral part of their socializing function. However, the stronger the black women's movement becomes the stronger so too will this aspect of their socializing role.

Nevertheless, in whatever ways women resolve these ambiguities, the women's movement can only be strengthened and enriched by diverse approaches and different perspectives. Dr Carroll maintains that through the recognition of the similarities and differences in the women's movement 'the black women's experience could add depth and meaning to many areas in the development of an understanding of "equal opportunities" '.

I want now to consider further women's history and its consequences for the school curriculum and the education of girls, as an example of the implications of the continuity/discontinuity dimension.

White history or women's herstory?

Girls grow to womanhood knowing about Florence Night-ingale, Grace Darling, the wives of Henry VIII, Boadicea and the great Victorian Age, but how many black women in British history will they have learned about? Will they ever learn about Sarojini Naidu who entered Cambridge at the age of twelve and later became governor of Uttar Pradesh? Will they ever learn about Nanny the Maroon Leader defying her brother Cudjoe and the British and holding out in her mountain stronghold until betrayed into surrendering? Will they ever know about Mary Seacole who worked alongside Florence Nightingale in the Cri-mean War? How many women in the forefront of the women's movement know about the contribution of black women to the suffrage movement?

Bell Hooks, in writing about Sojurner Truth's pioneering work in 'ploughing' a path for politically minded black women in America, has researched the way in which sexism and racism have informed the perspective of American historiographers. She raises a vital point, that, *white female scholars who support feminist ideology have also ignored the contribution of black women*. She cites contem-porary works, mainly American, but also some British authors. Amongst those specifically mentioned in this respect are Barbara Berg, June Sochen, Sheila Rowbotham, Barbara Decker and Eleanor Flexner (Hooks, 1981). In par-ticular, Hooks cites the case of Mary Church Terrell in June Sochen's *Herstory*. Dr Terrell was active in the suffrage movement in the early twentieth century, both in America and in Europe. In fact she went on a lecture tour in Britain and shared the platform with Nancy Astor, the first woman MP. Hooks maintains that Sochen misrepresents and reduces the political contribution and importance of Dr Terrell, by portraying her as solely concerned with the black American Rights Movement. Which version shall we teach our girls, or shall we continue to diminish or keep silent about the work of women such as these?

Despite centuries of racial imperialism, patriarchy and, for some, the experience of slavery, womankind has not only sustained its belief in its own worth but has fought determinedly to convey this belief throughout history. In so doing women have made a monumental contribution to humanity – unnamed, unsung, unglorified and undocumented. The contribution must now be documented in full for if history still continues to ignore the continuation of black women's struggles down the ages, their daughters will have to begin each time to struggle anew.

I wish finally to turn to the *practical* implications of challenging and overcoming the obstacles to the achievement of equality for *all* women and the part education can play in initiating and facilitating change.

General strategies

Materials should be developed which would aim at raising the consciousness of pupils from the primary level upwards about sexism in the media, books, learning materials, the curriculum and in society, at large. Furthermore, they should aim at helping pupils to analyse the social, economic, and psychological processes through which gender and ethnic roles are constructed.

Systematic work should be attempted to develop an understanding of patriarchy and racism as historic, systemic, social, cultural and economic phenomena in society. A special goal should be to create and develop an understanding of the unique role women have always played in forging humanitarian ideals and fighting for humanitarian goals alongside or in opposition to men. Attempts should be made 'to recover the lost and neglected history and culture of women of all classes' and in particular the contribution to history of 'women of colour'. (Moraga & Anzaldua 1981: Carby 1982).

Girls and boys should be given access to knowledge about women's contribution to society in war and in peace, the fight against discrimination and to developing the concept of democracy through the fight for women's suffrage. They should also be aware of the part women have played in the fight for human rights, justice and the many freedoms taken for granted today.

Specific changes to the school curriculum

A considerable body of research now exists which shows in which particular areas of the school curriculum girls have been either discouraged, demotivated or otherwise dissuaded from participating fully. (Sutherland, 1981: Spender, 1982a: Kelly, 1981). It will be necessary to develop a series of wide-ranging constructive measures to reverse these processes which, as we know, begin early and increase in scale and pervasiveness throughout a pupil's life, in and outside of school.

The following points might prove helpful in providing a challenge to the debilitating educational process mentioned above:

1. Certain schools are already monitoring girls' achievement and progress in science, maths and other technical subjects. This could be expanded in a more systematic, comprehensive and goal-directed way.
2. One of the main aims of such monitoring could be directed towards ensuring that the education service provides an adequate and attractive (basic) education in maths, science and technical subjects up to a level which:
   (a) prepares pupils to live and function effectively in a highly technological society.
   (b) provides sufficient basic grounding in science and maths at secondary level to enable girls to see the advantages of continuing these subjects to 'O' and

'A' level and the scope that doing so affords them in their ultimate choice of careers. (see syllabi in Danish and Norwegian secondary schools).

(c) provides counselling and support to black girls by showing them what the difference would be in the scope of options between science subjects and those subjects hitherto popular among them at secondary level. Unless they can be professionally advised about the difference in scope between those subjects which are and have been traditionally popular, and the possibilities of other choices, it is difficult to see any change in a pattern which has become predictable and stereotypical.

(d) The initiation of special projects for black girls thus bringing together both the recommendations of the Rampton Report (1981) and suggestions for greater sex equality in education.

3. There should be a considerable expansion in the development of curriculum materials which promote the understanding of the complexities of the patriarchal and sexist society in which we live and the many processes which help to socialize girls into acquiescing and participating in these processes. Teacher and pupil material is needed to raise the consciousness of pupils on issues like:

(a) the public construction and abuse of female sexuality

(a) the different beliefs that exist of men's work and women's work

(a) the pay differential that exists between men's work and women's work and that between black and white workers.

(d) the structure and mechanisms for controlling and determining pay.

4. We should explore the feasibility of having self-defence recognized and included in all physical education syllabi to enable girls to defend themselves and personal space in school. Self defence may also help to develop

qualities of discipline and self assurance which are likely to encourage girls to become more assertive.

Many of these suggestions could be regarded as good educational practice rather than of specific benefit to girls, whether black or white. However, I would maintain that anti-sexist and anti-racist practice *is* good practice.

In conclusion there may be controversy about ideology or about tactics which give rise to internal antagonism in the women's movement (Banks, O., 1981, p. 5). However, if the move towards equality is to succeed, women must work together. We must acknowledge and try to understand our different perspectives; for if, in the end, the women's movement tears itself apart, the effect for our children would be the same as if it never happened at all.

Recording the School Experiences of Girls

CHAPTER 5

Mary, Jane and Virginia Woolf: Ten-year-old girls talking

LESLEY HOLLY

> Above all, where is it leading us, the procession of educated men?
>
> (Virginia Woolf, Thirty Guineas, The Hogart Press, 1938)

Children are not thought able to understand the complexities of the social world which we inhabit. However, in this chapter I suggest that children, in this case ten year-old girls, often have an intuitive grasp of the social processes which mould their lives. In particular I argue that the girls I interviewed understand the nature of sexism but have not accepted its inevitability.

The long process of teaching girls their place in the world as domestic resource units, is one of the sub-plots of our education system. It used to be rather more overt. A report 'Half Our Future' in 1963 was able to rely on the comfortable bedrock of perceived normality.

> The domestic crafts start with a built-in advantage – they are recognizably part of adult living. Girls know that whether they marry early or not they are likely to find themselves eventually making and running a home.
>
> (HMSO, 1963)

This helped to justify the exclusion of girls from science, reserving scientific expertise for those who would participate fully in the world of work (Kelly, 1981).

Today the language of equality obscures the discrimination which girls suffer. Most headteachers will deny the existence of sexism in their school. But underneath, very little has changed. Because in most schools few attempts have been made to understand the nature and manifestations of sexism, it remains the constant organizing principle of mixed schooling. Girls are neat, boys are not. Boys are good at maths, girls are not, and so on.

For the girls in this study their understanding of sexism centres around their exclusion from football and the softer treatment they receive in the classroom. They have not yet accepted sex discrimination as an everyday and ordinary event. It will take the experience of a co-educational comprehensive to finish that part of their educational training! Eventually the social injustice of systematic discrimination against women will become accepted as 'normal' by them. Nonetheless, I will show that these nine and ten year-old girls are already aware of the sexism directed against them and actively struggle against this injustice.

The girls go to a junior school in a university town in the south of England. This is a school with which I was familiar and which I had visited on a number of occasions. I especially wanted to talk to the pupils as I had already interviewed the head and some of the teachers and attended many of the school functions. I am focusing here on the experience of girls in junior school because I consider this a neglected area of schooling. There has been a tremendous amount written about secondary schools and infants' schools have been the subject of recent interest (King, 1978). Junior schools are forgotten territory. They are somehow seen as marking time between infancy and adolescence. My own children found the transition from infants to junior school a particularly trying time and I knew from their experiences and my own partially remembered junior school days that there was an exceedingly abrupt change on leaving the infants. In the Junior School it is often the case that the child-centred education of the infant's school is no longer considered appropriate and discipline and hard work start to take over. (Ronald King interestingly portrays the pervading images of infants' schools and points to similar differences between infants' and junior schools (King, 1978)).

The school in this study has a male head and three other male staff as well as 6 women teachers, so it presents a contrast to the all-female staff of its neighbouring infants' school. Positioned by a main road, surrounded by shops and owner-occupier houses, the catchment area of this junior school is mainly white middle class. This is an area of relative affluence and employment in sharp contrast to many other parts of Britain.

Although the head and deputy head are men, all the staff on lower scales are women. In an interview the head expressed his commitment to 'a happy, well-run school'. And he feels that he has made some concessions to 'equality' – for instance, both boys and girls set the tables for lunch and clear away later. However, sexism *is* one of the organizing principles of the hidden agenda of the school. This is true for the women teachers, who do not get appointed to the higher positions in the school and who are encouraged by their male colleagues to be 'feminine'. The head remarked to one woman teacher in my hearing 'you look very nice today Miss Green'. She was wearing a skirt – a change from her usual garb of comfortable trousers and a sweater. She explained later 'he'd like all the women to wear skirts for school, but I'm not going to. They get tangled in the wheel of my bike'.

Sexism is also the organizing principle underlying many aspects of pupils' lives. Two summers ago the head decided that girls should no longer be allowed to wear shorts in the summer. Fortunately he was defeated by the fact that so many girls continued to come to school in shorts despite the demands that they 'dress like girls'.

I talked to a group of five girls after school on three

occasions. They were all in Mrs Hope's class – third-year juniors, aged between nine and ten. They seemed glad of the opportunity to talk about their lives. I did not know at the time what would emerge from these conversations and I listened to the tape recordings many times before I realized that the girls were giving me a powerful analysis of the tightening web of sex discrimination.

They told me something about themselves. Three said that their mothers stayed at home to look after the children and one of these was doing an Open University degree in psychology. The other two girls had mothers who were single parents in full-time paid employment – an art teacher and a social worker.

They soon got used to the tape recorder and I let the conversation drift from one subject to another. I tried to be unobtrusive and see what parts of their lives they would make visible.

Playtime certainly occupied a great deal of the conversation.

Mary: play is the best – We play bulldog and chain-tag. Sometimes we sit and talk.

Jessica: But the boys think they kinda rule the football pitch. You can't often play football. You might be able to play but you'd be very lucky if you would. Normally it's just the boys on the football pitch.

LH: Where's the football pitch?

Mary: We have to play in the middle and outside the football pitch. Sometimes we play down the side. Sometimes we don't play anything. We sit by the sides and talk about things . . .

So it became clear that the girls thought the boys took up the most space in the playground, and that they also perceived this as unfair. The rules relating to who occupied any given space may be unwritten and yet they reflect the society which generates the rules.

As Shirley Ardener explains:

Societies have generated their own rules, culturally determined for making boundaries on the ground, and have
divided the social into spheres, levels and territories with
invisible fences and platforms to be scaled by abstract lad-
ders and crossed by intangible bridges with as much trepi-
dation or exultation as on a plank over a raging torrent.

(S. Ardener, p. 11, 1981)

This applies to the school playground which in this case, is
an example of the sexual division of space.

Janie Whylde writes:

Most (playgrounds) are mixed now, with an area set aside
for ball games. This will usually be dominated by boys,
while girls congregate around the edges or in secluded cor-
ners.

(J. Whylde, p. 30, 1983)

Of course when I looked in the playground it was not the
case that the girls were passively huddled in groups. They
were also racing around but the boys had a large football
game organized and monopolized the main section of the
playground. This had the effect of restricting the girls to the
edges. The teachers and dinner ladies seemed to be quite
happy with this arrangement.

Mary: The dinner ladies don't think the girls should
          play football.

Neither does the school secretary. When I told her about
my interest in girls playing football she was horrified.

Mrs Bates: Why do you want girls to play football?
          Why not just let them be girls?

I tried to explain to her that the girls themselves wanted to
play.

These five girls had played football the year before with
their teacher and had enjoyed it. There is nothing intrinsic
about football which excludes girls. It is a game of skill and
speed, but it had become a rallying point for one kind of
male identity and girls are therefore systematically excluded.

Mary: Girls *can* play football (in the playground) but nobody's organized it, so that the boys think they should be able to play it more – that it's their football pitch and it's always going to be like that.

Jessica: It might be something to do with them going and playing on the field all the time (in the games lesson) for the football team.

Mary: We played football last year with Mr Jones, but that wasn't anything to do with the teams. That was in our PE lesson – it wasn't a complicated thing. Mr Jones said 'Come on, we're going to play football' and we just did it. It was good.

Pat Browne, Lene Matzen and Janie Whylde in an article on sexism in physical education explain the importance of teaching football skills to girls.

> When they (girls) play football, they get lots of encouragement from boys (as long as they don't have to play with them). They are learning to play the right sort of game, they are aspiring to something higher, but in the eyes of most boys they are still 'only girls'; an alternative could be to train girls very thoroughly in the tactical and technical skills.
>
> (Whylde, 1983, p. 279)

They point out the importance of building up the confidence of girls and, if this small group of girls is typical at nine and ten, they are still keen to learn to play and enjoy football.

However, football occupies a mythological place in our culture. It is the celebration of male skills and stamina and football matches are the arena for male competition and violence. One of the defining features of football is the systematic exclusion of women. It also monopolizes television space, playground space and reinforces substantial male ownership of many aspects of the environment.

The debate is not at all new, Virginia Woolf quoted from a report in the Daily Herald, 1936.

Official football circles here . . . regard with anxiety the growing popularity of girls' football. A secret meeting of the Northants Football Association's consultative committee was held here last night to discuss the playing of a girls' match on the Peterborough ground. Members of the committee are reticent . . . One member, however, said today 'The Northants Football Association is to forbid Women's football. This popularity of girls' football comes when many men's clubs in the country are in a parlous state through lack of support. Another serious aspect is the possibility of grave injury to women players.

(Woolf, V., p. 213)

It seems that women have been fighting this battle for decades. The reasons for prohibition have shifted however from fear of 'grave injury' to a less compelling argument about changing facilities.

The headteacher explained the system to me.

Girls can join in the training sessions but they can't play in the teams. It's an FA* ruling you see. It's to do with the changing facilities. Of course that doesn't apply so much at this age (junior school).

In any case a girl would have to be very good to play. We can't make any exceptions. We couldn't make it easier for the girls. They'd have to be really good and really keen.

*FA – Football Association

We have here an example of how an apparent policy i.e. equal opportunities, can handicap girls. Girls are allowed to play football but they have to go along to lessons and training sessions which are all male. The girls have to be better than the average boy because even those boys who are not 'really good and really keen' can still go to football training. The girls have to prove their worth whereas any boys can play football as their right. The girls must combat decades of disadvantages just to go to football practice. Though these girls play and enjoy netball they would like to play football as well.

Mary: Now we play netball – it would be fair if you
           could have a choice. To play (football) you have
           to have football boots and all the gear. I went and
           asked the teacher if I could play football and he
           said 'next term we'll see' and nothing really hap-
           pened.

Jessica: They say 'Yes you can play' *but they just kind of
           bear you.* They don't invite you.

Mary: We had a class newspaper. I wrote a letter and
           said 'Why can't girls play football?'

The girls feel that in some way football is used against
them. Jessica's poignant comment 'They just kind of bear
you' shows how it feels to be hardly tolerated rather than
completely accepted. The boys play the prestige sport and
have the space to expand and enjoy it.
Two boys who talked to me from the same class explained:

Tom: The girls used to play last year. But now we learn
           football skills and they've kind of dropped
           behind. They do netball.

Jamie: They were good last year. I liked those games.

These comments from the boys in the class suggest that the
main opposition lies in the stereotyped thinking
embodied in the school organization. This is contrary to
the views of many teachers who locate sexist attitudes of
pupils in the home. I suggest that this enables them to
ignore the entrenched sexism within schools.
    However, even though football is used against them, the
girls still feel that being a girl has its compensations. This
revolves around the softer treatment they receive from staff
and dinner ladies.

Karen: The dinner ladies are a bit silly. We fake we've
           hurt ourselves and they let us go inside. But it
           never works for the boys. They tell the boys to go
           and stand outside. They are much stricter on the
           boys. They hardly do anything to us. We don't
           get picked on by the dinner ladies.

This softer treatment for girls extends to the classroom.

Wendy: Mr Jones used to be horrible to the boys. He used
         to shake them by the hair and throw them into a
         corner.
LH: Were the boys really naughty?
Wendy: No, they were just talking pretty much the same
         as the girls. He favoured the girls more.

The rewards for being a girl are therefore quite obvious.
The girls are increasingly encouraged to accept femininity
in the form of protection as the source of their power. This
process is described by Jean Anyon in her study of three
schools in the US.

> Femininity is often used to achieve power in a situation or
> relationship . . . in which the male has power.
>
> (J. Anyon, p. 25, 1983)

Girls are encouraged to occupy the female role and are
rewarded by softer treatment in school. As pupils progress
from infants school to secondary the organization of
schooling increasingly begins to reflect the cult of mascu-
linity. The girls exclusion from football is only one mani-
festation.

The process has been described in detail by Dale Spender (1982). She writes about the problems of getting
educationalists to even acknowledge the existence of
sexism.

> If educationalists were to acknowledge this problem and
> tackle it, perhaps my criticism would be modified. But they
> do not classify this as a problem for it is not a problem
> for men. On the contrary many male educationalists con-
> tinue to deny its very existence and insist that equality of
> opportunity prevails even while one sex is so demonstrably
> dominant and at the expense of the other.
>
> (Spender, p. 199, 1982).

These girls in this junior school are being initiated into this
process of learning to be 'real' women. As Jean Anyon
points out:

This ideology of femininity reinforces a paternalistic dependency on *men*

(her emphasis, Anyon, p. 34, 1983).

Girls and boys *are* treated differently despite the head's belief in equal opportunities. The girls have an easier time but they are excluded from certain male preserves such as football and playground space. Yet this is but the tip of the iceberg, for eventually, in secondary school this will extend to limitations of subject choices and sports facilities. The girls are further taught their future roles by seeing the women teachers in the school in a subservient position to the men. These girls suspect, however, that the women teachers in their school do not give the head their wholehearted support. Their new teacher Mrs Hope is popular. But Wendy thinks she doesn't like the headmaster.

Wendy: I don't think Mrs Hope really likes him (the head). She makes faces at him when he's not looking.

Jane: I don't think any teachers really like him.

Wendy: Mr Maynard does.

Jane: Oh yes Mr Maynard does *because* he's the deputy head.

Mr Maynard, the deputy head, is a young man who is making his way up the career ladder. It is to his advantage to remain friends with his superior who appointed him and in due course will no doubt recommend him for a headship.

In pointing out this relationship between male head and deputy the girls are very astute. They know that young men are supposed to climb the career ladder and a recent news item in the Times Educational Supplement highlighted the furore which can occur when women seek appointments.

The headline was:

Protest over head's appointment

The parents have expressed dissatisfaction . . . at the governors' decision to appoint Mrs Gloria Peach age 46 to the Headship of Blewbury Primary School, a Church of England controlled school.
While they have no personal criticism of Mrs Peach, they say they would have preferred a young man in the job to provide a balance of age and sex in a school which will now be staffed entirely by women.

(TES, page 1, Friday June 24 1983)

A young man in authority over an otherwise female staff would have conveyed an entirely different message to the pupils. One with which these parents were in sympathy, we are told.

White middle-class men have a value in our society to which no other group can aspire. The ambition and careerism that young men so often are encouraged to display epitomize the deepest values of our culture – individualism, success and competition. I believe that our education system uses the language of equality as a mask for rewarding different groups unequally.

The girls I talked to have not passively accepted themselves as victims of a system which defines them as less naughty than boys, less deserving of the same amount of space and incapable of kicking footballs. They see the injustice of all this and they struggle against it. However, because being a girl means getting softer treatment they know that they have some advantages. As Jean Anyon shows in her work this turns out to be patriarchy's ultimate weapon.

A vision of a different kind is needed if schools are genuinely to provide equality; it would have to be co-operative, peaceful, gentle.

I leave Virginia Woolf to describe how this non-aggressive, non-competitive education might look.

What should be taught in the new college, the poor college? Not the arts of dominating other people, nor the arts of ruling, killing, of acquiring land and capital. They require too many overhead expenses; salaries and uniforms and ceremonies. The poor college must teach only the arts that can be taught cheaply and practised by poor people; such as medicine, mathematics, music, painting and literature. It should reach the arts of human intercourse; the arts of understanding other people's lives and minds and the little arts of talk, of dress, of cookery that are allied with them. The aim of the new college, the cheap college should not be to segregate and specialise but to combine. It should explore the ways in which mind and body can be made to co-operate; discover what new combinations make good wholes in human life.

(Woolf, V., p. 62, 1938)

or as Wendy, one of the girls, says more simply

Wendy: I think the class should work together no-one should go ahead. People boast, 'I'm on this page' but I think it would be nicer if they could work together 'cause then everyone could keep up.

These girls are not making points which are radical or uncommon. In undertaking similar discussions teachers might like to explore the experiences and feelings of their girl pupils. In doing so ingrained prejudice inherent in our education system might be exposed. The girls themselves need to be encouraged to work out ways of dealing with the sexism which they encounter. The most hopeful aspect of my conversations with girls is that at nine years old girls still notice sexism and it makes them angry. That is surely something to build on.

CHAPTER 6

Black Girls Speak for Themselves[1]

KATHRYN RILEY

Introduction

A key aspect of a feminist perspective in research is to make women visible in fields where they have previously been ignored or overlooked. Educational research which refers to students or pupils, frequently means boys and often white boys. Girls at school are assumed either to be non-existent or just pale reflections of the male pupils. Black girls are doubly invisible.

Removing the invisibility is not only a matter of studying the girls and drawing conclusions. It also involves letting them speak for themselves – giving them a voice and then listening very hard.

It is easy to assume that to find out about young black women all we have to do is to add up what we already know about young people, black people and women.

But any such piece of sociological arithmetic merely compounds the distorting stereotypes about those three groups and gives an answer that is woefully inaccurate.

The stereotypes are correct only in the sense that each group faces discrimination. Young people are increasingly being displaced from the labour market. Black people face discrimination in housing, employment and education. The gap between women's average hourly earnings and those of men is increasing rather than diminishing.

It might therefore be reasonable to expect that young black women realize that they are at the bottom of the pile, trebly burdened with discrimination. This was not true for the group of girls I talked to in an inner-city girls' school in South London. I did not tell them that they were supposed to be oppressed; they told me how they planned to organize and control their lives.

I talked to fifteen 5th and 6th form girls of Afro-Caribbean (Jamaican) origin in small groups over a period of several months. Their opinions came over strongly in three main areas. Firstly, they had firmly held and clearly articulated views on gender and sexuality. They did not consider themselves peripheral to male black culture, nor did they consider themselves to be passive sexual objects with little involvement in the 'real' male world. Secondly, they had a keen sense of political awareness and a determination to challenge political decisions which might restrict their future prospects. Thirdly, they were well able to analyse their own experience of schooling. Although a number of these young black women were justifiably critical of many aspects of this schooling, they were also able to evaluate, and use creatively, the more positive aspects of their school life.

In talking about gender roles, many of the young women challenged what is often considered appropriate behaviour for girls and boys at school. Each of the groups I worked with criticized the restrictive 'female' subject choice offered to them. One common demand was for woodwork:

> Woodwork, woodwork; there used to be woodwork but we don't even do it no more.

Many of the girls argued for mixed schools because they thought these would provide greater opportunities:

A chance to do metalwork, woodwork you know, and the
boys a chance to do needlework and housecraft.

They could not understand why it is, that in some mixed
schools girls are reluctant to do subjects like metalwork.
They argued strongly that they would not be reluctant to
come forward.

Several of the girls had been born in the Caribbean, or
had been educated there for some time, and were very critical about the rigid gender role stereotypes which are re-
enforced by an English education. For example, Valerie,
who was born in London but for several years, along with
her two brothers, was brought up by her grandmother in
Jamaica, comments:

> What's wrong with English education is that they don't
> learn the boys nothing about needlework or cookery. In
> Jamaica, the boys have to do needlework and cookery. For
> they think that if a boy don't get married, he's got to cook
> for himself. Like my brothers, well we used to live with my
> Nan, she was a bit old-fashioned, well she wasn't that old-
> fashioned because she let us out, but she thought that we
> should do our cooking and cleaning and she was right.

The girls clearly expected males to take an equal part in
domestic life. Many girls complained vociferously about
the laziness of their brothers. Valerie argued that this 'laziness' was a product of the English way of life. That in
Jamaica, men had been expected to help domestically, look
after their children and where necessary even bring them
up on their own. In Britain, Jamaican men followed the
example of English men and of their friends. Domestic
chores were considered 'unmanly'.

Most of the girls had very clear views about the role of
women and were highly critical of many current assumptions:

> Valerie: One thing about this country, they discriminate
> against women. Women aren't good enough to
> work in a coal mine, but in other countries,
> women join the army.

Sandra:	Like in this country, we'd never send a woman to Mars. In Russia, they sent that Maria to the moon or whatever.
Yvette:	I think men treat women really delicate.
Valerie:	Some men make out that you're going to crack if they just touch you. Crack, just like that.
Sandra:	But in Russia, a woman is capable of doing what a man can do.
Yvette:	And in Germany.
Sandra:	Yes, in those countries, yes.

On several occasions, the girls were quick to challenge what they thought were my assumptions. For example, I asked one group of girls whether, if had they gone to a mixed school, this would have encouraged them to apply for less traditionally 'female' occupations?

What do you mean by a female type job? I want to go in for pharmacy and they (the teachers) said it's a man's job.

Later on in the same group:

| Christine: | It's good if you're getting a job that men usually do. You're achieving something. |
| Annette: | I couldn't do that job of being a secretary sitting at a desk every week. |

Several of the girls wanted to do traditionally 'female' jobs, of which the favourite was nursery nursing, But these girls were no more 'traditional' in their attitudes than those who wanted to be pharmacists. Annette, for example, who had described secretarial work as being boring, wanted to be a nursery nurse. She argued that this would be far more interesting than any of the occupations suggested to her by the careers teacher. She explained that whilst she liked working with children, she also regretted the limited range of opportunities that her schooling had provided. She particularly would have liked to have done woodwork, but thought she was a bit old to take it up now!

In discussing Jamaica with another group, the girls were very dismissive of the particular West Indian paper I read: 'That's mainly advertising and beauty contests' was their comment. My rather embarrassed protestations that I read the paper because it had a good education column were considered to be irrelevant.

I asked a number of the girls to compare life in Britain with life in Jamaica. In doing this, the girls keenly asserted the independence of women:

Valerie: My dad, he wanted to go back. We'll stay here as long as she (my mother) wants.
Others: Yes, that's right.
Valerie: He (father) goes, he's got no life over here.
Others: That's what my dad says too.
Valerie: He says to his wife, 'Go and do this' and she won't do it.
Joan: Staying over here, he ain't got no control over his wife.
Others: They don't like it.
Valerie
  & Joan: Yes.
Valerie: They ain't got no control over the girls either.
Joan: Women can work over here, earn their own money, do what they like.
Doris: I do what I like.
Joan: Men object to that.

In terms of sexuality and relationships with the opposite sex these young black females totally negated the steroetyped idea that young females see themselves as potential dependents of men. Independence was something that they took for granted. As one girl replied, in some surprise that I should even ask the question, 'I mean, everyone wants to be independent.'

Most of the girls expressed a determination to get on with their own lives and argued that whilst relationships with men were important, these should not determine the course of their lives:

Valerie: Just because you get married, that's not an end of your career. I agree with them, you shouldn't give everything up for a man.

Education was the vehicle to achieve this independence. It

was a commodity, possession of which allowed females to enter into relationships with males on equal terms. In explaining this, the girls constantly referred to their mothers:

Angela: My mum, she thinks that you shouldn't get married too young because she married my dad when she was young and it didn't work out. She tries to tell me that you must have an education first before you take up your responsibilities.

Yvette: She say I must get a good education first, and then, I want to (get married). But at least get a good education and don't run wild and get yourself pregnant or something like that.

Sexual relationships were acceptable, but early pregnancy was to be avoided. It made life very hard, and could be a threat to independence:

Sandra: Because when you've got a child, you've got a lot of responsibilities and your education suffers a lot . . . Because my cousin, she was really bright at school and then she got herself pregnant by this boy who didn't care nothing for her. He wouldn't even own up that he was the father and so her education was spoilt. But my aunt took her back and said that she would take care of the baby and she would send her back to school to pick up, where she left off.

Other examples were given of young girls who had become mothers and had had a 'hard time', although in many instances, boyfriends had given a lot of help. No criticism or judgement was made about these girls, but one or two of the girls I talked to were highly critical of the 'English' response to pregnancy in young girls. Although early pregnancy was hard work, and a threat to independence, it also had its compensations and rewards. It was certainly not a reason to get married. This could only cause further problems in the future:

Yvette: Over here, if you have a kid and it's illegitimate, they say, 'You've got to get married. A disgrace.'

> They (Jamaicans) don't seem to think about it
> like that. It's just normal.

None of the girls felt that colour should matter when it
came to relationships, 'If you really care for someone, then
colour doesn't matter'. However, whilst expressing this
sentiment, they recognized and resented the double standard which operated. Black boys could go with white girls
but a black girl could not go out with a white boy:

> If you go up (the shops) and you see a coloured girl and a
> white boy 'ogging-up' and everyone is staring at them.
> And if it's a coloured boy and a white girl, everyone would
> just walk past.

The girls indicated that both parents and male relatives
tried to exert propriatorial rights over girls which they did
not attempt to impose on boys. Black girl–white boy
relationships seemed to break an accepted social code.

> They can't bear their sister to go out with a white boy. Or
> their cousin.
> He's a boy, he's allowed to have a white girl. You're a girl,
> you shouldn't do the same thing.

For these young black women gender and sexuality were
interrelated. They did not think of themselves as 'delicate'.
They would not 'crack' if touched. Any suggestion that
they might be fragile in any way was met with shrieks of
laughter. They were looking for relationships in which
they had strong financial control, help with domestic
chores and child-rearing, and opportunities to continue in
their chosen occupation. They saw themselves as strong,
economically independent individuals, willing to engage
in emotional relationships but on their terms, not male-
dominated terms.

For them, there was also no sense that politics was a
'man's' subject. They did not consider themselves to be
passive agents in their own personal lives and neither did
they consider themselves to be passive in the public world.

A number of the girls were critical about the extent to

which their employment prospects were being jeopardised by the policies of this Conservative Government. From their own experiences and expectations, they began to theorize about the political and economic effects of Government policies:

Audrey: I mean, there's a lot of unemployment in this country. I don't know about anywhere else, but I've heard there's a lot in this country. And there's a lot of cuts. I mean, Margaret Flatcher...

Isatou: Thatcher, Thatcher.

Audrey: Well Thatcher, whatever her name is, she the Prime Minister cuts down a lot of people's money and a lot of things like that. She even cut down the Olympics money. You know the money that usually get for training. And you know she says she can't afford to give them say £1,000 a year and then suddenly, the money drops from heaven or the sky and she wants the Olympics held in this country. So I don't see where the money comes from, see.

Angela: Plus when Labour was in power they never had the money to give the police a rise or the army a rise or anything.... But as soon as the Conservative Party came in, the army, they got a rise. They've all got a rise but the small working-class who work in shops and companies, they haven't got a rise...

Parental comments were used to re-enforce these arguments:

Sandra: They're (my parents) very angry about what Mrs Thatcher's doing for a start. Because she's cut hospitals. What's she cut hospitals for? We need them. And she's cut schools. She hasn't cut private schools.

Valerie: Those public schools where those rich kids go, she hasn't cut them.

Joan: It's probably where she came from.

Valerie: It's alright for her. Her kids have probably left school while we're still suffering trying to get through.

Through discussions with these young women, it became clear that they were determined to take control of their own lives. Many of them also possessed a political understanding which enabled them to analyse and challenge inequalities. For example, in the following extract, Sandra (aged 15), gives a sophisticated account of the structure of modern Jamaican society:

> When I went to Jamaica, they called one part, the rich part, 'up-town', and the other part, the poorer part, the ghettoes. And my aunt took us around the poorer parts to show us what it would be like to be poor, how you would live and how you would survive. And we went to department stores and the people dressed well and they didn't go bare-foot. In the ghettoes, they didn't have anything to wear. There was lots of money, it was mainly high-class people who lived there and foreigners, British people and things. They operated the system and that sort of thing.

Their experience of schooling was clearly very important to them. They suggested that it was more important for them than for their male peers. Once again, they referred to Jamaica to help me understand the reason for this:

> Miss, in Jamaica, the parents tend to say that the girls must really prove themselves that they can stand on their own two feet without the help of their mum and the father and the relatives . . . So that's why I think most of them stayed on to school, whilst boys got jobs like factories and farms because most of the jobs in Jamaica were farms and the boys did that whilst the girls stayed at school.

Those girls who had been to school in Jamaica were particularly keen to relate their often contradictory experiences. For example, on the question of discipline, Valerie and Carol had very different views:

> Valerie: There was this teacher, I don't think she really liked us. She let me stand out in the hot sun and I had a cold and it was really bad. And I was out there, drooping, drooping and my sister came out and she was really upset she was.

Carol: Well, I know some of the teachers in this school,
           they have lessons and the children don't behave
           themselves and the children swear to them. They
           should report it and I think it would stop.
           Because many teachers, they're not strict against
           their pupils. They should be stricter . . . (In
           Jamaica) if you do something like swear to the
           teacher, you have to stand before the Council . . .
           When you come up to the examinations and
           fail, then you have to tell them why . . . You have
           to take it seriously.

In England, the girls argued that unlike in Jamaica,
parents encouraged boys and girls equally but that the girls
had a greater sense of responsibility for their families. This
gave them a stronger commitment to education. Through
education, not only could they help themselves, but they
could help their families:

Sandra: The girls, they've got ambition, they want to do
           well. Their family, if it's really poor, that will
           encourage them to do well in their lessons . . . I
           mean the parents, they encourage the boys but
           they just don't want to do it . . . They've got
           friends and they are trying to prove that they are
           the same as their friends.

School for these girls had a number of positive aspects. All
of the girls were regular attenders, but this should not
necessarily be interpreted as an uncritical appreciation of
the education they were receiving:

Angela: I've missed school once. It was so boring. That's
           what I said to myself, I'm not going to miss a day
           off school again because there's nothing to do.
           You turn on the television and all you see is the
           baby programmes or some intellectual stuff.
           They don't have nothing good on television. It's
           not worth bunking school.

They would all have liked a broader range of subjects to
choose from, as I mentioned earlier. They were very warm

about their teachers, whom they saw as trying to do a good job. They had very much enjoyed the smaller teaching groups which had come through falling rolls and suggested that the ideal size for a teaching group was 10 to 15 pupils. In these smaller groups, they had benefitted from the kind of attention they had needed.

One girl, born and partly educated in Jamaica, in particular praised the sex education programme:

Sandra: Miss, in Jamaica, the girls they start to breed from 11 upwards. In England you don't, well, you don't start from an early age. And that's what our parents are trying to show us. Because in Jamaica they don't have sex education like we know. The parents only tell them at a certain age.

Valerie: Like when it's too late! (laughs)

Sandra: Yes, when it's too late. So in a way English education is good because they tell you the facts of life and the basics about what happens to you in certain situations. In Jamaica they go, 'If anything happens to you, you're a big girl so it's your own fault and you know what's right from wrong.'

In each group, we discussed the qualities which made a teacher 'good' or 'bad'. A 'good' teacher was described as one who was 'punctual' and who 'pushes you and encourages you'. Each group gave the same examples of 'bad' teachers and one of the worst examples is vividly described by Angela and Audrey:

Angela: I'll give you an example Miss. Miss X we had her for two years, the 4th and 5th Year we had her. Just look what she done. Just split us up in half she did. The ones who could do the work, 'yes, I'll give you 'O' level'. The ones she thought weren't able to do it. 'You're doing CSE.' And she never cared about the ones doing CSE. All she cared about is the ones doing 'O' level.

KR: So you were divided up, what in the same class?

Audrey: Yes, one group, the 'O' level, sat at the front of the class and the rest sat in the back of the class chatting.

I asked the girls how she had made the divisions:

Audrey: It's who she likes. If you are a big mouth who likes to back chat her, she chucks you in the CSE and if you're a softy, you know, listen and don't talk a lot, she puts you in the 'O' level. You know, I think that's how she done it.

Angela: Everytime you talked, you know 'Hey, so and so; you know, we couldn't talk because we were split up. CSE couldn't talk to 'O' level and 'O' level to CSE.

Audrey: We were sort of like that. Did you watch that film when we were in the 4th or 5th Year and they split the class up according to colour of eyes? (Referring to a film which they had seen the previous year, 'In the Eye of the Storm'.) . . . sort of like that, yes.

When specifically questioned about the division into 'O' level or CSE, the girls argued that they thought the division had been made in terms of whether you 'back chatted' or not. They did not think the decision had been based on colour. However, my own count of who had been placed in each of the groups suggests that most of the black girls had been placed in the CSE group.

We would condemn the classroom division into 'O' level/CSE on broad educational grounds alone. However, we must also condemn it for its racist outcome, even though this was not perceived as such by the girls themselves. They argued that there was little intentional racism in the school but quoted examples of blatantly racist attitudes in other schools.

There was one area, careers advice, in which a number of the girls suggested that less was expected of them because they were black. A range of concerns were expressed about the school's careers programme. The careers programme, which included an input from the School Careers Service, had not been systematic. The job information the girls had received had been narrow and had dealt largely with traditionally 'female' occupations, such as banking or secretarial work.

Several of the girls, who had not achieved good examination results in the 5th year, had made a particular effort to stay on into the 6th Form to improve their examination results and get a good job. They felt that several adults in the school had low expectations about the kind of work they were fit for, and that they had been discouraged by the information that they had been given and the way they had been treated. They were particularly aggrieved at the way in which they had been 'shamed-up' by references to their lack of qualifications.

> Isatou: She puts everyone off. She's another one pre-
>   judiced, isn't it? She seems like she wants you to
>   end up in Tesco's packing beans.
> Audrey: She sort of puts you off. That's why instead of
>   encouraging yuu to do something, she puts you
>   off. That's why most of the girls don't go to her
>   for advice about jobs.

It is quite clear from the context in which these remarks were made that the girls felt that this kind of treatment had been meted out to them because they were black. In this instance, they felt that the treatment had been racially discriminatory.

From the point of view of these young black females, careers education had not only discouraged them but had also failed to provide them with the 'hard' information that they had needed. The girls did not appear to be unrealistic in their ambitions and were very aware of the problems of getting jobs:

> Audrey: You go hunting everyday and you read every
>   single newspaper. My brother, he just sits there
>   at the telephone raising my mum's phone bills
>   and he still can't get one.

They also recognized that being black was going to make finding employment even more difficult:

Christine: It's mostly whites, whites do the jobs with the good qualifications. . . . They just put up some barriers, or make some excuses.

Angela: You can't get jobs. There should be jobs, but it depends on the employer as well. He might be one of those who doesn't like blacks. I mean, if a white person and a black person went to the same school and got the same degrees, the white person is more entitled to get it than the black. I mean, we're all classed as stupid.

Conclusion:

Angela's scepticism is well founded. She assumes that potential employers are male and white. She didn't need to be taught that it's a White Man's World. But it can be challenged, by teaching her to change it.

Note

1. This chapter is adapted from an article originally printed in *Multiracial Education*: Vol. 10, No. 5, Summer 1982.

CHAPTER 7

Mixed Blood – That Explains a Lot of Things: An education in racism and sexism

LEILA SULEIMAN & SUSAN SULEIMAN

Background

My daughter Leila was bright, and had been assessed as top of the class in her 11+ preparation examinations. A few days before she was due to sit her selection examinations, her father, my ex-husband whom I had divorced on grounds of violence, reappeared after an absence of several years. The effect of the visit put both of us into a state of extreme anxiety, with the result that Leila failed her examination.

In 1978, the Local Education Authority in the Outer London Borough in which we live was still in the process of reorganising Secondary Education on comprehensive lines. At this time, some parts of the borough had mainly comprehensive schools, while others had a mixture of selective, (old grammar and technical schools) non-selective, (old secondary moderns) and so-called comprehensives, which in reality took only children who were graded as lower ability at eleven years.

We were unfortunate that our catchment area of the borough contained most of the old selective schools and none of the true comprehensives. The one school which was offered to non-selective girls was the local mixed 'comprehensive' which took only the lower graded children. The school, with 1500 children, was set in the middle of a vast 1950s cottage-style council estate, on which I had grown up.

Although disappointed that Leila was not able to attend a real comprehensive school, we had hopes that the school might give her a good education and so, after much consideration, dismissed the possibility of appealing against her placement.

The first year

Leila started attending her secondary school in September 1978. After two to three weeks, the first-year children were assessed and graded. Leila's reading age under the Neale Analysis of Reading Ability was assessed as thirteen years, and her spelling age, fifteen years. She was consequently allocated to a class in the top band, where she had none of her former classmates from primary school, and was therefore separated from her close friends. New teachers, insensitive to racism, questioned her in front of the class on her racial origins because of her 'foreign' name. This focused on her the attention of a group of boys in the class who were young National Front supporters. In her own words,

Many of the boys in my class were National Front supporters. They used to chant National Front slogans i.e. 'Wogs out, N.F.' etc. with a raised arm salute, at regular intervals during the day, usually where I could hear them, and where it was not possible to get away from them, for example, in the classroom. The teachers never made any attempt to stop them. When I first joined the school, I was liked by the boys, but this didn't last longer than a couple of weeks, because once it 'got around' that I was half Turkish, and therefore unusual, they started to dislike me and their taunting began. A group of them used to pick on me in the classroom, in the playground and in the dinner queue, in fact, anywhere they could. Sometimes they would attack me, and every day, several times a day, boys used to punch me. I don't mean playful punches, I mean real ones.

At that time it was very fashionable to be a 'skinhead', and to adopt the skinhead image which is extremely 'macho', and the skin head attitudes to racism. (Although not all skinheads were racist, the people that I knew all were).

I used to come home in tears four out of every five days, because the day was just one long round of hassle and abuse, coming from all sides. There was one boy in particular who was the worst. He was quite big for his age and considerably bigger than I was (I weighed under six stone). He took a delight in being racist towards me and telling me that I should 'go back to Turkey'.

I have attempted to bring up my daughter with socialist, feminist and non-racist values, and an awareness of racism and sexism. Consequently, we developed a very open relationship, and we were used to discussing these and other political issues. This relationship allowed Leila to discuss the racist abuse she was receiving from the start.

What appeared to be happening from a 'political' perspective was what I would call 'ranking'. The boys, on entry into the first year of a large secondary school are 'at the bottom of the pile' and have no established position. In order to establish positions of dominance they jockey fiercely among themselves. Their methods of obtaining dominance include banding together in gangs, demonstrating physical strength and control over others by intimidation and violence, and dominating the arena of the classroom. Recent studies have shown that 'within the average mixed classroom, boy pupils attract 75% of the teacher's help and attention, dominating both lesson content and access to learning materials. (Val Millman, 1984a).

Leila was very outspoken and articulate and particularly enjoyed contributing to class discussions. She found that she was the only girl to do so. I believe that many of the boys, particularly the dominant group, saw this as a form of competition, and therefore a threat to their control. This belief is born out by studies carried out by Dale Spender (Spender, D. 1978), who has argued that mixed classrooms do not allow girls the opportunity to talk, even when teachers are keen that they should. She reports a conversation with girls at an ILEA mixed school in which it was claimed that it was unfeminine to talk. (Spender, op. cit.) Where boys would ask questions, make protests and challenge teachers, girls, even when they thought the work was silly or boring, would 'just get on with it!' (Millman, V. op. cit.)

The boys response to behaviour they considered competitive was to attempt to intimidate Leila with racist and sexist abuse, threats and physical violence. These techniques demonstrated very clearly to less dominant boys and to the girls what they could expect to receive if they 'stepped out of line'. Other girls avoided this attention by keeping quiet. There was one very intelligent girl from Turkey in Leila's class who was very quiet, but could not entirely escape abuse because of her racial 'handicap' and was reduced to tears in the class on several occasions by racist comments.

I wrote to the school to complain about racist language, and the physical violence that Leila was subjected to, but did not receive a reply. One morning, towards the end of the term, Leila was attacked by a group of boys during the chemistry class, and ran out of the school the two miles to my mother's home, where she arrived in tears and a state of collapse. Her absence that day was not even noticed.

My response was to write to the school, pointing out that she had been suffering racist abuse, which had culminated in this attack, and to ask for an urgent meeting to discuss the matter with the Head of Lower School. At this meeting, I was told emphatically that 'this school *does not* have a race problem!' They said that they considered Leila talented and were very pleased with the standard of her work. I described her isolated position and asked if there was any possibility of her being moved, or any of her former classmates joining her, and was told it would be considered. I heard later that one of her friends would be joining her class in the Spring Term.

At the end of the Autumn Term, Leila won the School's Creative Writing competition and her illustrations were published in the school magazine. Her report was excellent, with eight A's and two B's for Effort, (A=excellent, B=good) and for Attainment, eight 1's and two 2's (1=above average, 2=average). Her work was described as 'imaginative and highly original', 'her oral work very pleasing', 'considerable natural ability', 'excellent progress', 'makes a valuable contribution to the lessons'. Her attitude was 'always keen and enthusiastic', 'a very willing and pleasant pupil', 'a very helpful member of the form'.

The effects of the harassment were cumulative, and Leila became very anxious and depressed, crying nearly every night when we discussed what was happening. The anxiety began to trigger off repeats of the earlier obsessive behaviour she had displayed years ago. (e.g. frequent washing of hands) after witnessing an attempt by her father to kill me when I asked for a divorce, and after suffering for over a year, threats of violence and kidnap.

As a parent, I felt very impotent at her distress, and very angry that the school allowed this behaviour, refusing to accept that the problem of white racism existed, and taking it as a slur on the good name of the school that I claimed that it did. In this situation, I felt that to approach the school again would create a backlash for my daughter. At this point, I could only encourage her to defend herself verbally and physically to the best of her ability, and give emotional support by 'talking things out' and hope that the situation would improve. Shortly after returning to school after Christmas, Leila fell seriously ill with whooping cough and was absent from school for nearly a term.

In May, I was surprised to receive a letter of complaint from the school about her low output of work on a week's

school trip she had undertaken at the end of March.
Although I had had misgivings at the time, our G.P. had
said that she was fit to return to school. Subsequent events
showed that she was still suffering from the effects of the
whooping cough. I had been shocked by her state of health
when she returned home, and by her accounts of poor
supervision – staff regularly getting drunk, and eleven and
twelve year olds allowed to wander alone around a strange
town late at night, to drink alcohol and stay up late at dis-
cos. My first impulse had been to write to the school to
complain but, on consideration, felt that this would only
exacerbate my daughter's position.

Now, six weeks later and faced with a complaint from the
school, I replied, pointing out her illness and questioning
the quality of the supervision which had not identified
this, or her poor work performance. The school asked me to
attend meetings with some of the staff who were on the trip
and the new Head of Lower School. In the course of these
meetings, allegations that Leila's standard of work was
deteriorating were withdrawn, and instead, a complaint
that she was 'too different' from the other children was
made. It was explained that she was very polite and
hardworking, but that 'her attitude suggests that she does
not see herself as being subject to the normal requirements
of the class'. In my opinion, this referred to her practice of
discussing issues with adults as an equal, which some staff
found very threatening, but others positively enjoyed.

I suffered an inquisition about my personal life by the
Head of the Lower School – was I actually married to the
man that I lived with? She asked about Leila's father's
nationality and when I explained that he was Turkish, her
response was 'mixed blood – that explains a lot of things!'
Although usually quite an assertive and articulate person,
I felt humiliated and intimidated. She insisted that Leila
must cease to be 'different' (although it was never
explained what this 'difference' was) and must learn to be
like the other children.

The Head of the Lower School then set up a system of

detailed confidential reports to be made by Staff with regard to Leila's attitude towards staff, attendance, conduct in the classroom, dress and work performance. I was invited to the school to discuss them with her. The reports were generally favourable with 'good and fair work performance', 'well behaved and hardworking'. One member of staff noted that she was anxious. She was criticized for:– being 'demanding', 'very clinging if one wants attention', 'rather fussy', 'always wants her question answered first', 'needs a lot of encouragement before she settles down to work'. This behaviour was symptomatic of her anxiety state.

The second year

In the Autumn Term of her second year, the system of confidential reports continued. This encouraged Staff to focus attention on her as a 'problem', and some of them, particularly new Staff, saw this as a punitive exercise. She was now being harassed not only by pupils but also by certain members of Staff as well. One in particular, her German teacher, who kept pin-ups on the wall of his stockroom, insisted that she call him 'Sir' on every occasion, pick up litter which other classes had thrown down and repeatedly laid emphasis on her name. He kept her behind after class frequently, and on one occasion, asked her if there was 'any part of her that was English?!' She refused to reply. One of her tactics for dealing with these situations was to run out of the classroom and out of the school. Since she had a talent for long distance running, it was impossible for him to catch her. On one occasion, he resorted to confiscating her coat and bag, but this did not prevent her running to my parents' home. When the Head of the Middle School rang to say that she had left her things, she told him that she refused 'to be treated like a dog'.

At the beginning of the second year, one of the N.F. ringleaders had been transferred to a lower class because of poor work performance, but there still remained six boys who habitually harassed her. There were very few children from black or ethnic minority backgrounds in the school, the majority of the pupils coming from white working class homes on the surrounding council estates. Non-white children were consequently very isolated. In Leila's class, a large Anglo-Asian boy had aligned himself with the N.F. group, and although he didn't physically assault her, would chant N.F. slogans and racist abuse.

The general election in 1979 stimulated an increase in N.F. activity in the area and in the school. The constituency in which the school stood polled over five hundred votes for the N.F. candidate.

In October, I received a summary of the latest confidential reports from the Head of Lower School, and an invitation to discuss them. The reports complained of 'lack of attention', 'lack of interest', 'slow to follow instructions', 'slow written work', 'laziness', 'performance not up to standard'. I asked the Head to stop the confidential reports, as I considered that they were having a negative effect, and wished to allow things to cool down: I declined to visit the school to discuss them.

In November, one of her 'tormentors' walked up to Leila in the corridor and without saying a word, pushed her down a flight of concrete stairs. The result of this was a badly sprained ankle which was painful and crippling for several months. The previous January, she had entered for the Area Schools Sports cross country championships and came first. This January, she was unable to compete because of the injury. I wrote to the school, complaining of this, and assaults with stones, punching, kicking and spitting, but did not receive a reply. This was a very difficult time for Leila. Her anxiety was intense, and prevented her from concentrating, listening and absorbing what staff were saying to her. Her work and health suffered. Although she was up early in the morning, because she went through rituals of preparation, she frequently went to school late. She was always excruciatingly slow at getting ready to go out, or in carrying out any task. She became obsessively worried about dirt and germs.

I felt desperate, and looked around for another school, even visiting a private one, to discover that I couldn't afford the fees. In the winter, she again became very ill, with a bad case of measles. She was unable to eat properly, her weight went down to four stones and she was absent from school for six weeks. When she returned to school, she suffered from frequency of urination. I believe this was related to anxiety and her illness. The rules concerning the use of toilets were that pupils were allowed to use them only during the morning break and lunchtime. They were not allowed to leave the class, or use them between classes. The boys' toilets were left unlocked, which effectively allowed their use at any time except during class, but the girls' toilets were kept permanently locked, except for the morning break, and the first and last fifteen minutes of the lunch hour. I discussed Leila's problem with my G.P. and sent a note to the school to ask that she be allowed to use the toilet as needed, for medical reasons. This involved getting the teacher's permission to leave the class and going to see the Deputy Head of School, who held the key, and returning it to her. On one occasion, she asked her why it was necessary to lock up the girls' toilets while the boys' were unlocked.

When I attended the parents' evening in the Spring Term, I had a long wrangle about toilets with her Form Tutor, who informed me that it was character building for Leila to hold her 'water' and learn control! My appointments to see other staff were interrupted by the Deputy Head of School, who insisted on seeing me. She was shaking with fury as she poured forth a tirade about Leila having the audacity to ask her why only the girls' toilets were kept locked – 'I don't need a second year girl to tell me how to run my school!' During the following discussion, I explained about the harassment that Leila was subjected to and the anxiety she suffered as a result, and was strongly advised to take her to see a child psychologist. I had no intention of doing this, as I was aware that she would then enter the system, recorded as a 'problem child' and that this was yet another method of blaming the victim, that allows those responsible to do nothing about the real 'problem'.

That summer, Leila represented the school at Crystal Palace and became the under-14 Fifteen Hundred metres Champion in the Area Athletics Championships. Her success as the school champion in long distance events at school and in the Area Athletics brought her respect and a form of popularity. Her strange name, from being an object of abuse and ridicule, was chanted by the school at races, and her 'difference' earned her the status of a mascot.

The third year and after

In Leila's class, and in the school as a whole, the boys were in a minority. This was because, of the two non-selective schools in the catchment area, one was all-boys. The boys in Leila's class complained that they were in a minority, and the school took this complaint seriously enough to transfer them into another mixed class, at the beginning of the third year, removing an equal number of girls from that class into Leila's. When this swop took place, the first girls-only class was created, (although by default.) The effects of this were extremely beneficial, and harassment from boys virtually ceased from then on.

There were still conflicts with certain staff, particularly her Form Tutor and the Deputy Head, that persisted throughout the school, but Leila was able to deal with these quite effectively with assertion training techniques, after coming on a course with me, and reading relevant books. Despite adverse predictions, she left school after the fifth year, having gained five 'O' levels, one of the very few pupils to do so. She is currently studying English, Government and Politics and Art 'A' level at a College of Further Education. I know that her current achievements are far short of her potential, and that she has paid a very high price for being herself.

Strategies for survival

Looking back, I feel as a parent that I made mistakes in my approach, but also found some positive strategies. I was naive in my belief that the issue of racism would be taken seriously, and in not realizing that my daughter would suffer a backlash as a 'troublemaker' for daring to name what was happening to her. I would advocate caution to other parents, unless there is a teacher you know you can trust, or other parents with similar problems who are prepared to join you in approaching the school as a group.

Parents have very little power in this situation, and must use what they have to support their children. Making it possible for the child to talk through her experiences freely and with confidence, and putting what is happening in a political perspective helps to release tension and de-personalize attacks. It is most important not to blame the child, or collude with teachers in blaming the child, which they will pressurise you to do. Keep a record of all letters from the school, reports, letters you send and notes of phone calls for reference purposes. Don't allow your child to be officially labelled as a problem child by agreeing to send her to an educational psychologist. Encourage her to defend herself physically and verbally against attacks, even if this is seen as 'unfeminine'!

My experience is that schools of this type do not aim to educate children, i.e. help them realize their full potential, encourage them to exercise their minds to the full and become creative self-aware individuals. Instead, they effectively reduce their aspirations, so that they will accept their station in life, and not compete with middle-class children for professional jobs. The whole ethos of this school is conformity to stereotypes. Boys must be tough, and 'like boys'; subject to corporal punishment; allowed to wear 'bovver boots'; skinhead haircuts and army jackets. Girls must not wear trousers at school until the fifth year, however bitter the winter. They are, however, allowed to wear make-up and jewellery, and when in fashion, skirts slit up to the thigh! They can wear high pointed-toe stilettos, but not flat open leather sandals during sweltering summer weather. Boys must wear their blazers at all times during the summer, unless given permission to remove them by the class teacher! The work of good, enthusiastic teachers is outweighed by the bad, who allow racist and sexist comments and behaviour to take place without reprimand and in some cases, encourage it by their own example. The Staff in positions of power and authority as Heads of year and Head of the School claim that racism doesn't exist, and so allow it to flourish unchecked to the detriment of all pupils.

CHAPTER 8

Breadwinning and Babies: A re-definition of careers education

VAL MILLMAN

Introduction

A 30-page report published by the West Midlands Low Pay Unit in March 1984 showed that six out of ten women in the region earned less than the Council of Europe's 'decency threshold' of £100 a week. It concluded –

> It is evident there is widespread exploitation of female labour. The degree of anger and frustration expressed demands a concerted effort and response from those in a position to improve the quality of women's working lives.

In the City of Coventry, the prospects for female school leavers are particularly bleak. By the end of 1983 almost twice as many 16-year old boys as girls had found jobs totalling only 14% of the 5144 fifth-year pupils who had left school in the summer (Coventry City Council 1984). The girls' jobs were clustered in a narrow range of 'women's work', one-third of them in clerical and secretarial posts which are rapidly disappearing with the introduction of new technology.

Coventry also has an increasing number of teenage

mothers who have created, through motherhood, a form of status and responsibility that was unavailable to them through life on the dole. A mother in her early 'twenties in Coventry, who has been unemployed for most of the time since leaving school said:

> I wanted to get pregnant because I couldn't cope living at home. I wanted something of my own. So it was a way of getting out and I knew that the Council would have to rehouse me. A lot of people think that round here, several of us did it in my street because we wanted to get away. My family weren't bad. We were just overcrowded. Five out of seven girls in my street got pregnant without being married. Two got married later. And we all got council flats nearby. Life's easier on my own, I was lucky to get away.
>
> (B. Campbell, 1984)

Turning traditional assumptions upside down

Individuals, families, communities and institutions are currently having to undergo radical changes. Girls and boys, men and women are devising new ways of coping with the insecurity of the present and the uncertainty of the future. Despite a shortage of resources and government exhortations to return to Victorian values it is possible that these changes provide us with the opportunity to turn traditional assumptions upside down and develop a girl-centred approach to careers education that will also do much to enhance the lives of boys.

About three-quarters of all girls leave school at the end of their fifth year, many of them experiencing a chequered pattern of work illustrated in detail by the three examples below. This pattern has been typical of women's working lives for years but it has been ignored by school careers programmes which have usually focused on the uninterrupted career of the white, middle-class male. Sadly it has taken unemployment to raise questions about the assumptions upon which so much of careers education has been based. Clearly psychological theories of vocational choice (Kant and Browne 1984) are unable to embrace the social and economic factors which today determine the patterns of individuals' lives. As Linda Clarke argues,

> Careers can be regarded as developing into patterns dictated by the opportunity structures to which individuals are exposed, first in education and subsequently in employment. Individuals' ambitions in turn can be treated as reflecting the influence of the structures through which they pass.
>
> (Clarke, 1980)

This chapter does not attempt an explicit critique of traditional careers education programmes. Nor does it predict the exact shape of a radical alternative. It simply invites readers to explore the relationship between 'careers' and 'opportunity structures' to which three young working-class women have been exposed, and to consider the extent to which their ambitions have been shaped by social and economic factors – past, present and future. Although none of the three has become a teenage mother, 'N', 'J' and 'M' depict a range of experiences typical of their generation and common to all young women irrespective of differences in regional and ethnic background. While ethnic differences indeed exert a crucial influence, discussion of these young women's ethnic backgrounds will be postponed until later in the chapter. In this way, it is hoped that readers will focus on the impact of gender on *all* girls' lives rather than allow stereotyped assumptions about cultural customs to colour the detail painted in the pictures.

Good careers education must have as its basis a realistic rather than mythical perception of young people's needs. Studying the girls we teach and the young women we work with is the best way of achieving this; through a closer knowledge of their lives we can begin to construct a profile of factors which should be central to careers education. We can also begin to reflect on the very real part each of us plays in shaping girls' futures – 'Careers Lessons' simply bringing into focus the collection of messages we have given girls about 'womanhood' throughout the course of their schooling. (Millman, 1982, 1984)

Examples of three young women

Example One: 'N'

N is currently in the Upper Sixth Form following 'A' level courses in Sociology and English and an 'O' level course in Government and Politics. She lives at home with her mother and stepfather, (a taxi-driver), three younger brothers and sisters, and her elder brother and sister-in-law who have recently got married. N's father died when she was six. She also has two sisters, six and eight years older, who both moved away when they got married seven years ago.

N has experienced conflicts between school and family responsibilities from early childhood and has frequently had to take time off school to fulfill family commitments. When she was seven her mother took her out of school for a few weeks to stay with her elder sister who was having her first baby. Now, at nineteen, N has to take her youngest brother to the doctor's every week, regularly missing her 'A' level sociology class.

Her mother has been suffering from depression since N's elder sisters moved away and N has had to take increasing responsibility for the three youngest children. At first she didn't mind this, but when she moved into the third year and was asked to do more homework, she began to fall behind in her lessons. She was continually tired at school, falling asleep in lessons, and unable to get any 'thinking' work done at home.

> Sometimes I'd be sitting down and have to get up every ten minutes to do something. The little disturbances in the evening are never ending and then, when all the jobs are done, it's 'when are you going to bed?' And then I have the children in my bed if they're crying at night.

N's elder brother had helped her choose her subjects for her fourth year in secondary school. In addition to compulsory English and Maths, she chose Physics and Chemistry, French, Textiles and Dress and Computer Studies. Her parents showed little interest in N's school courses compared with her brother's, although her mother was quite angry to discover that N's Careers Teacher had advised her to take Computer Studies – she didn't think it would come in handy in the future.'

N began to 'turn against sciences' in her fourth year. She found that 'they needed more concentration than English which you have been taught since you were small, and computer studies was continuous assessment which I couldn't keep up with.' During her fourth year N stopped eating properly and she realized that she couldn't cope with the demands being made of her. Her elder sister discussed N's problems with her teachers who subsequently tried to offer N more support. N was allowed to sleep in the school medical room in afternoons, received regular health checks and had long discussions with a senior woman teacher who unfortunately 'seemed very strict so that I wouldn't dare ask for anything'. So, most of the time, N kept her worries to herself, shutting herself off from problems at home, 'trying to be as happy as possible at school'. But she didn't feel she was getting anywhere; she spent most of her time thinking 'if this . . . if that . . .' and frequently thought of DOING SOMETHING to end her problems.

At the beginning of her fifth year circumstances finally pushed N into taking a drugs overdose. Her mother was away visiting relatives in Pakistan, the family was living in temporary accommodation while their house was improved. One morning N had arranged for friends to take her younger sister to school as she had to get there earlier than usual. Her sister had an accident getting off the bus and had to undergo an eye operation in hospital. N was blamed by all her relatives for not being with her sister at the time.

N could not get to sleep that night because she 'felt so angry about everything'. The next morning she took thirty of her brother's asthma tablets. She became ill at school, was taken to hospital, staying there for several weeks before moving to a convalescent home and later to her sister's for the months it took her to recover. N was keen to return to school to re-take the fifth-year course. She is now much closer to her mother and receives more support from school – but the conflicts have not disappeared. N desperately wants to go to university but her mother, aunts, sisters and sister-in-law say she should leave school, get married and THEN do what she wants. N says:

> I think it's too late then – they're putting pretty pictures in front of me. I should be able to manage both school work and home if I'm properly organised.

N loves her parents and respects the Muslim way of life so that she finds it difficult to go against the wishes of her parents. At present she gets so confused about her future that she finds it difficult to concentrate on her 'A' level courses. She says she wants the chance –

> to learn, to make myself clear what I'm capable of doing.

Example Two: 'J'

J lives at home with her father who is a retired fork-lift truck driver, her mother who is a part-time nurse, and her younger brother. Her two older brothers and elder sister have all left home.

It took J three years to obtain her first paid job as a clerk in a small engineering firm. Nobody in the family had expected her to find work easily because 'they saw the unemployment figures in the news and saw riots and marches on the television'. J's parents are thrilled that she now has the sort of job she wants, and she didn't 'take just anything that was there'.

J had wanted to become a typist from her third year in school when her mother had bought her a typewriter.

Typing and Drama were the two subjects J had been best at in her fourth and fifth year and she has found both of them useful since she has left school. She left the school fifth year with seven good CSEs and went on to take a Business Studies course at the local Further Education College. She obtained a distinction in typing and she particularly enjoyed her work-experience placement which she had been nervous about beforehand. She had expected,

> the boss to be a man with a cigar in his mouth shouting at you – but it was a lady and things were different.

The only thing she didn't like about the College course was compulsory PE – because

> I haven't got a very good figure.

J looked forward to leaving college to 'starting off on my own and making decisions for myself', but she was unable to find a job to go to. She spent nine months on a clerical training scheme for the unemployed, doing much the same as at college, before getting a six-month work experience placement with a local electrical firm. Here J gained in confidence as she was carrying considerable responsibility and dealing with the public. Her placement was extended for a further three months before she was told there was no hope of a permanent job becoming available.

During the next four months of unemployment J spent most of her time looking for jobs. She had twelve interviews and turned down one job offer – selling encyclopedias on a commission basis of payment. Now she is thoroughly enjoying her first job which involves stock-checking, typing, switchboard duties and taking orders. She has already asked for a wage rise and earns £50 for a forty-hour week. She says she still gets less than,

> the two salesmen who don't do as much work as I do. Sometimes they boss you around and say 'go and make us a cup of coffee, love'. Sometimes I will, sometimes I say 'go and make it yourself'.

> Sometimes men customers come in and see Ron (the sales-
> man) standing there and think he's the boss. And when
> he's not here they ask for him. They don't really need Ron,
> they could easily tell us what stock they want and I think
> they think just 'cos I'm a girl I can't look for stock. And that's
> my job – it makes me mad!

J can't see any chance of further training or promotion with this firm. The only step up would be to salesman(!) and 'Ron wouldn't like that'. But she would like to become a 'manager or a boss in the future' or try a better-paid 'man's job' like building, bus driving or engineering'.

At present J is quite satisfied and enjoys the independence her wages give her. She goes out more than she used to and doesn't have to help out so much at home. She has a boyfriend and still sees five of her old school-friends. She thinks that

> most of the others from school are not working now, some
> of them are married, some of them have got kids and some
> have emigrated because they can't find work here.

J's elder brother has emigrated to Jamaica because her parents say, 'unemployment doesn't cause the same sort of trouble there. The young people can always help out their family on the farm'.

J expects to be married by the time she is twenty-one. She has started to put money aside as her mother does and she thinks there will be a better chance of getting a house if she is with a man. She looks forward to having children and hopes that she will be able to put them in a nursery or with a friend or her grandmother so that she can carry on working.

Example Three: 'M'

M had been on three youth training schemes before she got her present job as a clerk with an insurance company. When she was offered the interview it was for another work experience placement so she –

phoned the man up and stated if there's no job at the end of it, I'm not coming. I'll work for a month and if you don't think I'm suitable, tell me then.

Fortunately it became a permanent job paying £45 for a forty-four hour week doing clerical work and dealing with insurance claims by telephone and over the counter.

M had not known what sort of job she wanted to do while she was still at school. She had thought of nursery nursing but decided she wanted to earn money as soon as she left school rather than go on to further training. She had particularly enjoyed Child Care at school because she 'liked little kids then and all my friends were in it'. Now, at nineteen, M says –

There's a few like me – wanting to live my life and travel rather than spend my money on a house and kids. But most of my old schoolfriends are all having babies and getting married, – well, perhaps not getting married.

M is under a lot of pressure from her family, friends and people at work, to get engaged to her boyfriend. But she is in no hurry to leave home. Although her father, a long-distance lorry driver, has always been very strict with her, thinking M is going to 'get raped' every time she goes out of the door, he now 'gives her' quite a lot of freedom. She goes out most evenings and weekends, doesn't have to look after her younger brother like she used to and has saved up enough money to go on holiday with her boyfriend.

When M left school with 6 CSEs (having failed Chemistry and Biology) she went on a clerical training course for the unemployed because 'there was nothing else really to do'. Although she had gained confidence on the course, saying 'I used to be quiet but I'm a great laugh now', she felt that most of it was a waste of time:

You knew you were out after six months – they were just using you. As one left, the next one came.

When she was called for interview for other work experience placements she 'wore jeans, a leather jacket and flat bulky shoes, so that she wouldn't be offered them'. But she went on two more training schemes and was unemployed for thirteen months before getting her present job.

M is satisfied with her present work although she feels she is badly paid compared with Kevin, a young man of the same age who works with her.

> The customers often ask to speak to Kevin. He says just the same as I do, but they think he is right. I've got to accept it, ain't I, or I haven't got my job. I do just the same as Kevin except he sometimes tries to get me to do things for him.

The only way M could get promotion is if Lynn, the oldest 'office girl', left; it is unlikely because 'her husband has been on the dole for four years – he's really bored. He does the housework for her'.

Although M would like to earn more money so that she could go out by herself and pay out of her own money rather than her boyfriend's, she can't see the point of worrying too much about her job because –

> I s'pose I'll have kids one day and once a woman has kids she gets involved in the house. It would be good to get back afterwards, but how many of them do? SO WHAT'S THE POINT?

The influence of the girl's shared experiences

Nazish, Jenny and Mandy were all born in the same area of Coventry and were in the same form at secondary school. The population of the mixed comprehensive they attended was composed of 40% pupils from families of Asian origin, 40% of European origin, 10% of Afro-Caribbean origin and 10% from other origins. The three girls had been friends from the first year, although they haven't seen much of each other since leaving school, spending most of their time with friends from the same ethnic background. Occasionally cultural differences had divided them at school. Mandy remembers how hard Nazish used to work in lessons –

The Indians used to get most of the attention because they wanted to learn. We didn't. Half of the white people don't bother.

(TES 13.4.84)

Nazish had never been allowed to go to the youth club with Mandy and Jenny but the three of them remained close friends in school and they shared many experiences.

The girls' experiences at home and the 'hidden curriculum' of the school had clearly influenced their aspirations and their expectations of their future. To take second place to men and boys seemed the inevitable order of things, and they had had to devise a variety of strategies to deal with inequality both at home, at school and at work. They had also learnt to deal with both racist and sexist abuse, sometimes confronting it, sometimes ignoring it, more often learning to suffer in silence.

Although Mandy and Jenny had both gained confidence at work and on training schemes, they felt there was little they could do to stand up to 'the top knobs who are always men'. They had both experienced being dogsbodies for male bosses and invisible to customers, but they knew they must remain both pretty and deferential to 'keep the boss happy when he is in one of his moods'. So many of the feminine qualities and interests which had been nurtured since the primary school only served to reinforce their powerlessness in such situations.

Each of these young women felt that their domestic roles at home had been training them for their futures as wives and mothers. This had been at the expense of both school and career interests. None of the girls' parents had shown much interest in their school subjects, Mandy and Jenny choosing traditionally female subjects in their third year, Nazish moving towards the Arts subjects in the sixth form. However much Jenny might like the idea of moving to a 'better paid man's job' she will find it extremely hard to succeed with no appropriate exam qualifications. Each set of parents had treated their sons differently from their daughters – they took their school work more seriously, gave them more personal freedom, did not expect them to take the same responsibility for domestic tasks and took more interest in their future careers. The girls were all aware that male members of the household carried the ultimate authority and they expected to be married to men who would fulfill a similar role.

Although they had all looked forward to a greater independence when they left the school fifth year, few of their hopes had been fulfilled. Mandy and Jenny had succeeded in freeing themselves from housework and child-minding by going out to work and earning enough to go out in evenings and at weekends. But with little job security and few promotion prospects they realized that, in the future, they would continue to be dependent on parents, boyfriend or husband. The three young women all expected to be married by their mid-twenties. Both Mandy and Jenny already had 'steady boyfriends' but no marriage had yet been planned for Nazish. Mandy was under more explicit pressure to marry at the age of nineteen than either Nazish or Jenny. She was hoping to postpone marriage by earning enough money to retain some independence. Nazish was seeking her independence by staying on at school and later hoped to move away from home to follow a course at university. But none of them could talk of future career plans without reference to marriage, motherhood and childcare arrangements. How many school careers programmes currently address themselves to these sources of conflict and uncertainty in girls' lives?

Learning to overcome barriers to personal achievement

Nazish, Jenny and Mandy had all taken part in a three-year Careers Education programme receiving individual subject choice counselling in their third year. Each of them had maintained close contact with the Careers Officer after leaving the school fifth year and had received regular notification of youth training scheme places, college courses and job vacancies. In a sense they were the lucky ones. Their positive experience of school and their good relationships with teachers had enabled them to make good use of 'the limited opportunities to which they were exposed'. They had, at least, secured a tentative foothold in Further Education and the 'women's end' of the job market.

But these young women will need more than a 'tentative foothold' in an insecure and low-paid corner of the labour market to sustain them in the future. And it will take more than subject choice counselling and job information to give them this sustenance. While some factors clearly lie beyond the influence of the school, these three examples highlight many areas of school life over which we, as teachers, have control and in which we can participate. Each of us has responsibility for the future working lives and careers of the girls we teach. Not only must we seek ways of extending the limited opportunities offered to girls in both primary and secondary schools, we must also equip them to handle conflict and uncertainty with confidence and overcome barriers that threaten to stand in the way of personal achievement.

The success of our re-definition of careers education will depend on our understanding of, and commitment to, the future needs of girls and the prioritization of their needs in the construction of the school's curriculum. Central too will be our confidence in the resources of the girls themselves, a confidence which can free us from dependence on traditional approaches and resources, and ensure that we only use these to support and service our newly-defined careers curriculum. Secure in the knowledge that we are providing girls with knowledge and skills which will be of genuine assistance in adulthood, perhaps we can overcome our traditional fear of introducing problems and conflicts to young people while they are still at school. On leaving school all girls will inevitably have to learn to deal with conflict, uncertainty and even hostility. Surely it is preferable to assist them in this process, to anticipate and understand difficulties in the relative security of the school. If we, as teachers, continue to avoid this sometimes uncomfortable task, we should not be surprised to hear that many young women interviewed today remember Careers Education 'as a complete waste of time' (Bennett and Carter, 1981).

SECTION 3
School Accounts and Action

CHAPTER 9

Anti-sexism as Good Educational Practice: What can feminists realistically achieve?

FRANKIE ORD & JANE QUIGLEY

Implementing anti-sexist education involves change: a long and often painful process of changing people, changing ourselves, and changing institutional procedures and structures. Change involves an uneasy balance between conflict and consensus – between moving too fast or too slow, between taking people with you or leaving them stranded and antagonistic. We recognize that power is not given up easily but is fought for both within the individual (raising consciousness) and when confronting institutional sexism. But we also recognize that we live in a deeply sexist society and what we can achieve within our schools is dependent to a large extent on how legitimate the issues are seen to be amongst colleagues, the education authority and the state.

This concept of change as balance is important in other ways too. Sexism must be confronted in both the hidden curriculum and in the actual organization and content of what is taught; we must work both at consciousness raising and at changing educational practice; we must share our time between working with teachers and working with students. Do we concentrate on formulating whole school policies or focus on small, sometimes trivial issues? When do we take on the more contentious issues, for example sexual harassment, or male discipline procedures, and when do we opt for 'safer' issues, for example, registers in alphabetical order or girls wearing trousers all year. (Though having said this we are aware that in some schools all anti-sexist issues are 'hot'!) There is no one answer and each school will find its own 'balance for change'; but a recognition of the complexities of the struggle should guard against a rigid adherence to the notion of a *correct* formula.

Before considering in more detail how change has been effected in one London school we want to make a few general comments that are applicable to our school and hopefully more generally also.

It is very important that anti-sexism is seen as good educational practice rather than as an isolated or peripheral issue. It is too easy to dismiss gender as the concern of a few frustrated left wing women and to see girls, along with blacks, as a problem to be placated with the odd concession. Eventually we do want to see gender and race as legitimate approaches to educational practice so that in a consideration of, for example, option choice, mixed ability, the role of talk in the classroom, – the perspective is anti-sexist and anti-racist. However, there is a long way to go before this situation is likely to be the case.

In the meantime, one way we can avoid being marginalized is by operating through already established school structures. If schools have for instance an academic board where curriculum decisions are made, then anti-sexist recommendations should be considered here and justified in terms of general educational principles. Similarly tutor meetings, faculty meetings, staff association meetings are the proper forums for anti-sexism to be raised. Gender must always be seen as a school issue not a minority concern. After all, the underachievement of half the school population – even if it is only the girls – can be emphasized as a legitimate area for teachers and educational institutions to consider. If the ultimate goal is real structural change in schools rather than cosmetic tinkering then a first step is surely to avoid the 'working party mentality' approach where interested or partisan groups organize on the periphery of traditional school structures able only to make the occasional foray into the real power base. Rather, we have a powerful case to put to schools and we must present it 'centre stage' . . . This, at least, has been our experience.

Stress is an increasingly recognized feature of teachers' lives and obviously taking on anti-sexism is not going to decrease it. As teachers, we face daily onslaughts on our egos, and our confidence just from the nature of our job. We are also often tired and as a profession chronically short of time, resources and money. We need therefore to develop strategies to minimize the likely negative effects of attempting to implement anti-sexist practices. A working party or support group is very important here, as is setting realistic, short-term goals and enlisting the support of 'popular' figures within the school.

Firstly, *a support group*. Without the active encouragement of other people the familiar syndrome of failure, resentment, giving up, is only too possible. It is frightening how quickly we run into hostility or dismissive amusement when even quite small changes are suggested, and facing such reactions alone can be a daunting prospect. As we commented earlier, it is as well to be aware before beginning, that power is not given away, that there will be conflict and that we need to be prepared for it. Opposition takes various forms: aggressive personal attacks, the raised eyebrows of 'oh no, not this again', the stereotyping of one or two members of staff as 'the equal opportunities people'. In this situation a support group is both a retreat and a base from which to launch further initiatives. It is also useful to remember that there are sources of support outside the school. Groups such as WedG (Women's Education Group), magazines like GEN (the journal of WedG), and CASSOE (Campaign Against Sexism and Sexual Oppression in Education – a newsletter) provide a wider network and can prevent individual school groups from feeling isolated and insignificant. Equally important is that a support group can help us keep a sense of proportion (see Appendix for details). It should be a place where we can laugh at ourselves, at our mistakes and see that we don't take ourselves too seriously. It is essential to avoid the seige mentality where school – and life – becomes a grim battle against a hostile world. One of the strengths of the Greenham Common women is that they come across as real people – warm, funny, human. And no one can doubt their effectiveness and commitment! We don't have to be martyrs or fanatics; in fact, the earnest crusader is often her own worst enemy as she wears herself out emotionally and physically while alienating even the potentially sympathetic. Developing anti-sexist strategies in schools is important, and we are committed to it. But it doesn't encompass the whole meaning of life, and our successes – and our failures – need to be kept in proportion.

Which brings us to the second strategy for success – the *setting of goals*. Nothing is more debilitating than constant failure, especially after an enormous amount of effort has been expended. We found that the sense of confidence gained from winning several small concessions was a source of strength and a basis for taking larger initiatives. Again, there is a temptation to minimize what we've achieved; it looks so paltry when compared with what has to be done. But we need to keep a sane awareness that institutional change is almost imperceptible and that hundreds of years of patriarchal dominance is not going to be overturned in our lifetime.

Lastly, if possible, it is very useful to have the support of one or two *key members* of staff. With depressing frequency implementing anti-sexism in schools is still the prerogative of scale one and scale two teachers who often lack experience and almost certainly lack power. Effecting change under these conditions is really an uphill battle. However, the situation is changing. Increasingly equal opportunities is becoming a legitimate educational interest and although this has obvious dangers – you can kill an initiative or revolutionary movement as effectively by absorbing and neutralizing its energy as by opposing it – it also has possibilities which must be grasped. For instance, the appointment of Equal Opportunities Advisers in some Boroughs and the establishment of Equal Opportunities posts within schools means that Equal Opportunities is becoming a career possibility. This has two repercussions for feminists in schools. On the one hand, it means that Headteachers, Faculty and Year Heads, Chairs of Staff Associations etc. can be more easily persuaded to see the expediency of anti-sexist issues. Secondly, it gives committed feminists an opportunity to get into positions of power themselves. There's a lot to be said for pulling from the front rather than pushing from behind: at least it makes a change!

We began this paper talking about balance and this concept applies also to relations between feminists working together in schools. We want to avoid the all too familiar spectacle of the left tearing itself apart over internal differences. There is no one right way forward and we should adopt a flexible and conciliatory approach accepting that there will be variations in style, beliefs and practices and allowing people the space to work in their particular way. What follows now is an account of how, from these general principles, one school has begun to develop anti-sexist practices amongst staff and students.

One school's experience

Brondesbury and Kilburn is a split-side London comprehensive in Brent. It is a social priority school of 800 pupils and 60 staff. It is largely a working-class school of girls and boys, and is racially mixed. For the last three years we have been battling against possible closure and falling rolls.

We began in 1977 with our own lives. A number of us became increasingly irritated with the school administration's persistent use of the Miss, Mrs. titles, despite our wishes. Irritation grew to anger, first from the liberal belief that our right to be referred to in the way we wanted was being ignored; then as consciousness developed, we realized that these titles were symbols of a society which defined women according to their relationships with men (either you had one or you were still waiting!) and that this said something important about our position of power. The issue was raised at a staff meeting when a popular and erudite Deputy Head linked the discussion to the wider oppression of women, to the lives of Jane Austen and Charlotte Brontë and to the educational experience of his daughter. The staff was gripped. Many women, who at previous meetings had always remained silent, gave their support by referring to their own lives. The vote was overwhelmingly in favour of the use of Ms. when a title was deemed necessary.

However, the vote was translated to mean that women staff members had to inform the school secretary if they wished to transgress from the normal Miss/Mrs. position, hence labelling themselves extremists. Although a significant number of women did 'sign up', we were not organized enough, or indeed confident enough, to challenge the official interpretation.

Still, important change had occurred. People who trivialized the issue before the staff meeting certainly did not wish to, or dare to, afterwards. The intellectual tone of the discussion meant that for as long as most of us stayed at the school, it would be difficult to sneer at feminism. Although we didn't all argue for the introduction of Ms. from the same viewpoint, for the first time we did experience some female solidarity.

In fact, it was not until 1982 that the school officially adapted Ms. as the norm for female teachers. However, exercise books, minutes, school brochures, even staff meetings reflected the acceptance of the new title well before this date.

By 1982 a number of significant changes were occurring both inside and outside our school. The growth of the women's movement, a much increased awareness about sexism in society generally and for us in Brent, the appointment of Hazel Taylor as Equal Opportunities Adviser, all gave status and 'legitimacy' to our case. Inside our school, several feminists occupied powerful positions; a Deputy in charge of the Curriculum, a Head of Maths, Head of Fifth Year. Most significant was the new Chair of the Staff Association, a popular and strong feminist who was elected unopposed.

We took up the issue of sexism almost immediately. Several of us planned a 'mini' campaign both to increase staff awareness and also bring about much needed curricula change. Forever conscious of the danger of being dismissed as 'strident, male-hating and humourless,' we produced a leaflet which included jokes and cartoons, as well as quotable quotes, relevant statistics, discussion questions and an invitation to attend a staff association meeting where an articulate feminist was to speak, and wine and cheese would be served. We distributed the leaflet to all faculties and year groups so discussion would take place before the meeting.

Our choice of speaker was good. She began with a series of factual and statistical slides which demonstrated that sexism in schools was not the product of over-heated feminist imagination. Her cool, reasoned delivery convinced those members of staff which a more impassioned polemic would have failed to reach.

A lively discussion was followed by the setting up of the inevitable Equal Opportunities Working Party which represented all faculties. We reported back to the staff association two months later with a paper which argued for short-term practical changes; for instance that registers and class lists be alphabetical, that girls be permitted to wear trousers all year and that the option system be changed so that Home Economics and Technology were not placed 'back-to-back.' Though well over half the staff voted in favour of these proposals, only the last one became official school policy at once, due in part at least, to the feminist Deputy Head in charge of curriculum. The other two met resistance of a kind which is both depressingly familiar and difficult for ordinary teachers to combat. We were told that school uniform is the responsibility of the governing body to legislate on; we had to wait for an agenda short enough to include our item . . . as for the registers, a Department of Education and Science ruling apparently made it impossible for us to re-organize them alphabetically. We pursued this ruling – the famous Form 7 – and as expected it proved easy to overcome. In September 1983 all registers were listed alphabetically.

Light headed though these victories left us, no one would suggest that we were moving at a heady pace. Nor that our changes were radical. However, the organ of progress had been the staff association, and as its aim was to be the voice of the ordinary teacher, we moved only as far as people were prepared to go. Meetings had to be well attended for decisions to be listened to by the hierarchy and – finally – implemented.

Our only real power lay in our collective voice. Therefore, though sexual harassment and the possibility of organizing single-sex groupings in certain subjects were raised in discussion, not enough powerful voices were prepared to be allies in taking these issues further.

Changed consciousness about language stemmed from this time. The Ms. debate had emphasized the symbolic power of words and in public meetings throughout the school, teachers made a concerted effort to use 'she' as well as, or instead of 'he'. Terms like 'headmaster' and 'chairman' became, apart from the occasional lapse, obsolete. What happened behind closed doors and cupped hands is difficult to say, but broadly speaking, brochures, work-sheets, internal exam scripts followed the language norm we had defined; and once more one of our strengths was the Deputy Head who was in a position to keep a vigilant eye on all faculties' written work.

And so, despite huge compromises and a snail's pace, we finished 1982 feeling that progress had been made in small, immediate steps and that change was at least possible.

In June 1983 our school committed itself to anti-sexist and anti-racist practices during a day conference where we were formulating overall school aims and objectives.

Yet despite the magnitude of these commitments, little was happening on the feminist front. The debate had been moved off centre stage to the wings of a working party, where discussion continued, but out of the eye and ear-shot of most of the staff. Perhaps some teachers assumed too that sexism as an issue had been dealt with and that it was time to move on to the next educational fad. Perhaps also some of us needed a rest . . . For a while, we closed our classroom doors and carried on work there, rather than in the more conflictual atmosphere of the staffroom.

Towards the end of 1983 we entered our present phase. We reconvened the working party, encouraged more teachers to join from a wider faculty base and gave it the more combative title of The Anti-sexist Working Party.

We wanted to use the network of meetings already set up rather than to create a whole new plethora of our own. We were also determined that in a school which paid lip ser-vice to good education equalling anti-sexist education, there should be full staff involvement. Anti-sexism was not to be a hived-off issue for a few half-crazed enthusiasts to tackle; it was and is the responsibility of good edu-cationalists.

With these aims in mind, we presented a report to our curriculum planning body which recommended that anti-sexism be included on the agendas of all year and faculty meetings, and that each Head write a report outlining what had been tried so far in her/his department and what was envisaged for the future. Their reports are now ready for circulation and in a joint meeting between the planning body and the working party early next term recommendations and priorities will be established.

We used the third year consultative evening, an established and popular event, to begin a dialogue with our parents. We worked with tutors and pupils to produce displays which put a strong feminist case. We used pictures and photographs, statistics, charts and quotable quotes which teachers and students alike thought appropriate. The Women's Education Group (WedG) an organization based in Inner London helped us to find suitable pamphlets to hand out to parents. Tutors, who had already established firm contact with their parents, gave them out.

The evening was most successful; we had used a meeting already calendared and had worked with other members of the school.

Recently several of us attended a discussion on Sexual Harassment organized by WedG (mentioned above). We were impressed with the short film shown *'Give us a Smile'* and thought its every day pithiness, its cartoon form and its relevance to experiences of women would make it suitable material for sixth-form female students. Sixth-form tutors have agreed to work with us in running a half-day conference on Anti-sexism for pupils. They have also agreed to single-sex groups for this occasion.

Currently in pairs we are investigating a particular area of concern in the school. Careers, sex education, P.E., the language of reports, our ignorance of arranged marriages, examination results are all being considered from a gender point of view. Once reported on, findings will be taken to a staff association meeting and recommendations placed in the hands of the decision-makers.

Simple practical strategies have included the setting up of notice-boards in prominent positions and as part of the general area reserved for the Staff Association. We now have a reading area for teachers to browse through the endless amounts of literature we have received. A member of the working party is responsible for labelling the material and for sending reports of a specific nature to the appropriate department.

Our personal development and our own lives have been of considerable concern. We recognize the danger of committed teachers becoming burnt out, losing hope and energy, especially now when more demands than ever are being made of us. We try to keep ourselves afloat by celebrating any success, by inviting outside speakers to talk to us, by including reports from any courses or conferences attended (and by always making wine *et al.* available at our meetings). Articles of general feminist interest are circulated frequently and our other female Deputy Head is remarkably efficient about informing us of relevant courses.

There is a different mood now; a united group meeting in formal and informal working situations is less apologetic in its approach; consequently the response is more antagonistic. The balance is tipped towards conflict rather than consensus.

Alongside work with teachers, we will conclude with some examples of what has been tried with our students . . . We have taken the experience of two year groups and one faculty.

A year ago, first- and second-year tutors conducted an investigation into how students saw themselves and their futures. This was done through a diary entry set at a future date and a questionnaire. They also monitored teachers' classroom language, the oral participation and seating arrangements within the classroom, the use of playground space, corridor behaviour and the number of female and male students involved in the Compensatory Department. The results were as expected and left little room for complacency. One of our brightest second-year students saw her future as 'waking up to the twins crying and yelling . . . nagging to Fred as he runs to work in a hurry . . . going to the shops'. She commented on her day 'a normal day, nothing interesting happened'.

Boys were seen to demand and receive far more teacher time in the classroom in keeping with Dale Spender and many others' findings (Spender, 1980).

As a result of these investigations, the tutor team made various suggestions about the best way of giving a fair deal in the classroom. They included cutting whole class discussions to a minimum, breaking the class into small groups for talk and learning wherever possible; monitoring time spent with the students in the classroom and being firm about spending equal amounts with all students.

Though fourteen teachers from a variety of departments agreed to these suggestions, they were never put before an entire staff meeting and therefore have not been widely implemented. It is interesting to note though that the English Faculty has drawn similar conclusions.

First- and second-year tutors now use morning tutorial periods for single-sex discussions. The school's reserve tutor system (teachers who cover for absent colleagues) is used for the remainder of the pupils. During these twenty-minute periods, much is discussed not least sexuality and the way young females are taught to regard their bodies. The graffiti of the school has provided a good starting point.

One measure of change is the great increase of female students who now approach their tutors for informal chats about their bodily image. They are also much more likely to ask for help in removing offensive graffiti – feelings of shame have diminished.

The fifth-year pupils have been confronted with anti-sexism in a different way; a symposium was held where tutors invited various community-based organizations such as the National Abortion Campaign, Women Against Violence Against Women, The Brook Advice Bureau, the National Council for Civil Liberties, to lead discussions. This was the first time that tutors and students had seen the value of single-sex groupings, especially for girls. It was a positive learning experience for many of us.

As an example of faculty initiatives, we include the report written by the English Department for the Curriculum Planning Body mentioned before.

The English Department's strong commitment to anti-sexism and anti-racism is on the grounds that good educational practice necessarily involves providing all students with equal access to all knowledge that the school deems valuable. We recognise that anti-sexism must be confronted on two levels: the overt curriculum content and the hidden curriculum, for example, classroom organization.

Generally speaking, we think that making gender a 'topic' is a less useful method of approach than thinking of gender as a perspective on work in English. The former approach can too easily lead to the 'we've done women in the fourth year' mentality so that sexism is seen as a problem like capital punishment, abortion, the generation gap, etc. Approaching gender as a perspective on English teaching also means that we can use traditional classroom readers usefully. For example, we can ask such questions as;

– how many of these novels are written by women?

– how many have women or girls as their main characters?

– how many contain examples of positive, well-balanced relationships between boys and girls?

– how are mothers and fathers portrayed in these books?

Examining the stock of class readers with these questions in mind might reveal distinct gaps and imbalances in the overall picture pupils are getting of femininity/masculinity from 'official' classroom reading. Again, looking at particular books in detail can provide instructive examples of how sexist stereotyping operates in books. Focusing on a book from the position of the female characters is another way of challenging or revealing the sexist assumptions implicit in many of our class readers.

Below are some suggestions for classroom practice which were adopted by the department:

Firstly, *seating arrangements*. It was felt that a variety of seating arrangements can be adopted to suit the tasks set in the lesson. Mixed groups and single-sex groups within the class can both have a positive function. Secondly, *teacher style*. Up front teaching militates against girls as boys demand and get more teacher time. Generally the faculty supports lessons which involve small group work. Thirdly, *role play with role reversal* can be of particular benefit to students. If the students really adopt the role they can cross sexual divides. This is also a useful technique for studying class readers. '101 Dalmations' is a wonderfully different experience for students when Mrs Pongo becomes Pongo! Finally, teachers need to work hard at encouraging the assertiveness of girls, and ensuring that girls get a fair share of teacher time.

Other small but significant gains are; books are chosen with strong female characters; we've joined Letterbox Library (see Appendix); drama lessons with role reversal often take place; classroom tasks are allocated equally to male/female students (i.e. girls operate video, help move furniture); individual teachers have worked on topics related to gender. For example, women's images in the media; workbooks, looking at class readers from an anti-sexist stance have been produced in collaboration with the Brent Curriculum Development Support Unit.

This initiative has enabled us to work with teachers from other schools and has also meant that technically the finished product is of a very high standard. The first of these booklets on 'Summer of my German Soldier' is currently being piloted in four Brent schools.

For the future we plan to extend and develop initiatives we've begun, in particular concentrating on finding more suitable literature for classroom use and making the presentation of women a central theme in our media studies programme.

Conclusion

It is obvious that considerable change has occurred at Brondesbury and Kilburn, but how to evaluate what we have achieved is a more complex problem. Psychologically there is a tendency to swing between euphoria and depression depending as much as anything else on the sort of day we've had! More importantly perhaps, our political perspective also determines criteria we use to evaluate the importance of the changes we've made. We think we have achieved some significant organizational and procedural changes: the anti-sexist working party meetings appear on the official school calendar; Home Economics and Technology are no longer back to back; non-sexist language is the norm in all school correspondence; we have begun to monitor our school leavers to see if there are significant differences between what happens to girls and boys after school.

It is much more problematical assessing changes in attitudes, image and self-esteem. It is our impression that girls at Brondesbury and Kilburn are less invisible than they used to be. Tutors comment on girls' increasing assertiveness and expressed concern about sexist graffiti or verbal sexual abuse from the boys. Girls are more confident in English orals – they will more readily contradict the boys or assert their right to have single-sex groupings for discussions of 'sensitive' issues such as rape, arranged marriages, abortion. Although difficult to quantify, such changes are nevertheless of the utmost importance.

To end where we began: with ourselves. We know that as people, as women and as feminists working at Brondesbury and Kilburn we now have a more intelligent and profound awareness of the nature of patriarchy and how it oppresses all women. We know that this knowledge has increased our confidence and determination to confront and oppose the oppression. And of no less significance are the firm friendships we have formed amongst ourselves as we have struggled to effect change.

CHAPTER 10

A School Experience: Implementing equality in a mixed comprehensive*

BATTERSEA COUNTY WOMEN'S GROUP

In attempting to improve the education and confidence of girls in recent years two different perspectives have emerged. One has been concerned with developing an anti-sexist approach to schooling, based on the belief that women are oppressed by men and need to develop confidence and strength to fight against that oppression. The other has been more concerned with developing equal opportunities for both boys and girls. This second view maintains that boys need to be encouraged to be more caring and thoughtful about their roles as fathers, whereas girls should be given greater encouragement to go into careers which they have previously rejected or been rejected by. The fundamental difference in power relationship between the sexes has often been missing from this approach. Furthermore this second approach to change has been the most widely adopted since, in our view, it

* This article is the product of the contributions of six members of the group.

restricts itself to school issues rather than addressing itself
to a wider discussion of the unequal nature and structure of
the society. It is thus far 'safer' and more politically acceptable. (See Chapter 1 for a development of this analysis)

In Battersea County School, an alliance has been formed
between staff holding different perspectives in order to
achieve the greatest change possible within the school.
What follows is an outline of some of the changes that have
been made.

Six years ago we formed a small group of 3 or 4 women
teachers and tried to come to terms with the debates within
the feminist movement and our own position as women
teachers. We decided to think about the implications of
sexism in schools for ourselves and our students. Two of us
made a video in which girls themselves talked about their
experience of uniform, teacher attitudes, curriculum
expectations and the way they were treated at home compared to their brothers. This heightened our awareness as
well as those of the girls involved. We also became aware
(and extremely angry) about both the patronizing attitude
of many of the male teachers and pupils to our work and the
exclusion of girls from many areas of school life.

Over the next three years we managed to change certain
areas of the curriculum, especially English and Social
Studies and we also managed to rearrange pupils' names in
the register in alphabetical order. (Many of the women
teachers became known as Ms., rather than Mrs. and Miss
in order to prevent definition of women teachers on the
basis of marital status). At that time we found that we
gained personal strength from belonging to a small
women's group within the school. We were, however,
often ridiculed and seen as prudish, sour faced and bitter
women by many of the male teachers, as well as some of the
other women, on the staff.

At the end of this period we felt that we needed to
expand our sphere of influence and we therefore encouraged the Head to sanction the formation of a mixed Equal
Opportunities Committee with one representative from

each department. He was less hostile to the idea as a result of pressure from the EOC and the newly elected ILEA who were sympathetic to equal opportunities issues.

This newly formed committee took on the development of a whole school policy. We were given space to talk about the issues of sexism and gender at staff meetings and undoubtedly reached a wider audience despite the fact that a significant proportion of the staff remained hostile and cynical.

The different perspectives represented in the committee have resulted in tension and open hostility on occasions, such as when we invited a women's theatre group to perform to a girls-only group. Concern was expressed about the exclusion of the boys by some members of the equal opportunities group. However, on certain issues, more has been achieved as a result of the unity of a larger group of people, especially in terms of a critical look at resources and the wider curriculum.

We shall now look in greater detail at some of the achievements and changes within the curriculum which have taken place in the last three years.

Firstly we include a general review of changes made, followed by interviews conducted with some of the women involved in the Equal Opportunities Committee. Differences in perspectives and emphasis are apparent. Secondly we look at some of our attempts to tackle sexism in the 'hidden' curriculum. As well as attempting to change the content of what is taught within the school, we also felt that it was important to look at the hidden messages and assumptions associated with our behaviour and actions in school. Also, in this article we focus on one or two girls-' or women's-only activities. These were provided to balance the number and quality of activities available for girls and women in a school where most of the courses and clubs were traditionally dominated by boys or men.

The curriculum

Language and Images

The Equal Opportunities Committee examined resources used by each department and analyzed the materials in terms of their underlying assumptions about men and women. We came to the following conclusions:

(a) In many texts and classroom materials (especially for Maths and Sciences) females were excluded.
(b) Many books still assumed that the entire population is male by the exclusive use of the words Man, Mankind, He, Him, His etc throughout.
(c) In certain areas, especially in Textile Arts and Domestic Science, stereotypical roles of women and men were prescribed.
(d) In certain subjects, eg. Maths, there still appeared to be an attempt to appeal more to the interests of boys by quoting examples of male-related interests eg. football, fishing.

It became apparent from this survey that both the wider content of many lessons was sexist and that the notion of gender, if indeed it had been mentioned at all, had been referred to only in passing.

The extent to which the wider content of lessons has changed to date has depended upon the specific personnel within the department. Not unexpectedly, departments which have women who are deeply concerned about the issues have moved further more quickly. Moreover the process of change has not been one of evolutionary progression – rather of short jumps forward at specific moments in time and then possibly two steps back if teachers have left and been replaced by others less committed.

The following are responses from women from a variety of departments about if and how changes have been made.

(The extent to which the individuals interviewed represent their departments as a whole varies greatly.)

Science – Rowan

In the Science Department we have particularly concentrated on encouraging our girls to take up the physical sciences and to realize their potential in these areas. A science subject is compulsory up to fifth year in this school, but when it comes to third-year choices, the majority of girls appear automatically to opt for Biology – despite their previous enjoyment and success in the other Sciences. We feel this choice puts them at a disadvantage when looking for a career, as well as meaning that they may lack certain skills necessary for life outside school.

We have put considerable effort into ways in which we can counteract sexism in Science and the classroom.

1. Because I am also responsible for Careers Education I have been able to emphasise Physics and Chemistry as more viable subjects as regards career choice.
2. Internal exam papers have been altered so that in most cases scientists are now referred to as 'she'. Resources were examined for sexist pictures and statements and, although we did not have enough money to change them, it became policy to alert pupils to sexism where it occurred.
3. Photos were taken of girls doing experiments which were then displayed in the Careers Department and by some Science teachers. We also displayed posters of female Scientists, obtained from the Equal Opportunities Commission (See Appendix for Resources).
4. Sexist comments by pupils were dealt with by both the Head of Department and the pupil's Science teacher. The pupil was not, in general, admonished but rather taken aside privately and gently reminded about the fallacy of making such statements.
5. The progress of every third-year pupil was discussed

individually at Departmental Meetings and then counselling sessions were organized with many of the girls;
looking closely at their skills, successes and ideas about
the future. On discussion we found that girls, when
encouraged, often wanted to take Physics or Chemistry
for positive career reasons, or as a consequence of a
feeling of achievement in the past.

6. We have made efforts over the past few years to make
lower school courses more relevant to everyday life.
They are now more practically based, and the girls have
been given particular encouragement to achieve the
same levels as the boys.

7. In Physics lessons a particular attempt was made to
spend time with the girls, rather than allow the boys to
'take over'. It became (painfully) obvious that this was
extremely difficult to do and required immense determination from us as teachers.

Finally we decided to group all the new fourth-year Physics
girls in one class, so forming a single-sex group. We justified this by arguing that girls needed the confidence to succeed and also that the girls lower down in the school
needed to see that 'girls did Physics'; both were more likely
to occur in single-sex Science groups (Smith, 1984).

Maths – Jane

In many ways the introduction of a school equal opportunities policy had very little effect on the department. This
was mainly due to the lack of interest of members of staff
which meant that any reasonable discussion at departmental meetings was impossible. However, several changes
were achieved. One of the main reasons for this was an
increase in the number of women maths teachers and, curiously enough, their lack of posts of responsibility. This left
them much freer to work to their own priorities.

As a result of the general heightened awareness about
anti-sexism and equal opportunities within the school,
male teachers began to become aware of some of the issues;

and also that they tended to consult another male, rather than female, teacher when they had a maths problem. Now some male members of staff are making a point of asking questions of female teachers, particularly in front of pupils.

In the department we use a work card scheme, which is, at the time of writing, being vetted for sexism by a group of teachers from other local schools. Until now the choice of work cards and how they are allocated, has been left to individual teachers – but we are now spending a part of each departmental meeting going through work cards and discussing possible problems facing pupils when they do them. This, we hope, will highlight the need to give extra attention to girls when they are, for example, faced with a work card about cricket scores or football results. In the worst cases we intend to replace the offending card with one of our own.

Integrated Studies/Social Studies – Linda

In this department we have introduced the concept of gender to the pupils in the first year. Pupils have been given an introduction to stereotyping and gender roles through books and videos. Throughout the next three years they will re-encounter discussions about the issues through a variety of materials and subject content.

In the third year a major attempt has been made to make connections between gender and other concepts such as class, race and politics, as well as incorporating it in other elements of the course. Pupils who go on to study social studies/sociology in the fourth and fifth years spend almost a term looking at gender in considerable depth.

I believe that our attempts to keep issues of sexism at the centre of discussion throughout our pupils' school lives has been a major step forward – but at times we have faced difficulties from the apparent alienation of boys. Whilst politically one might adopt the perspective that more time should be spent encouraging the girls, in practice to have boys in the classroom is likely to present a problem, unless thought is given to materials presenting men in a less stereotypical form. Again, the best teachers did a lot in developing new resources and consciously thinking about classroom practice; the less committed did very little.

Computers and Computer Studies – Jane

Computer Studies is seen as a 'boys'' subject, both in our own school and more widely. This is evident from the greater percentage of boys opting for the subject in the third year in ILEA schools. (The situation is exacerbated by the fact that considerably more men teach computer studies than women). However, in 1983, many of our third-year tutors actively encouraged girls to choose the subject. As a result, for the first time, more girls than boys chose Computer Studies and care was taken to make sure that each class had a majority of girls. Even so, this caused a number of problems.

Boys monopolized the computers and teachers allowed this practice to continue, often leaving girls to get on with their written work. As a result of complaints by some of the girls, a meeting was held between the computer studies teachers, the head of year and the tutors concerned. It was agreed that teachers should note in the class register each occasion when pupils used the computer, thereby monitoring the situation – so that teachers would become aware of their own unconscious discrimination in allocating computer time.

A further development was the establishment of a computer club for girls only. As with computer studies, the mixed computer club run after school was dominated by boys (and was run by a man). Girls who *did* show an interest were obliged to climb over the boys' backs in order even to see the keyboard, let alone use it. Although, so far, there has been no huge take up of the girls' computer club one small group meets regularly each week. A further problem of resource allocation will arise later when more girls start to get involved since they will then be competing with the boys for the same club resources.

As a result of criticism by women members, the Maths department has begun to question the value of computer studies as an option subject and the suitability of the Maths department to run such a course.

In my view the emphasis on computer studies as an academic subject is the result of the dominating influence of men, who see computers in terms of careers development and high intellectual achievement rather than an everyday tool to be used by everyone.

English – Jackie

Within the department one or two of us have been consciously attempting to make our English teaching less sexist. We have looked closely at our set texts and, for external exams, have ordered books recommended as nonsexist by the English Centre, (particularly those which have girls as central figures). This we feel has gone some way to redressing the bias of our class texts which tend to have male 'heroes'.

We have many 'themes' and in revising them have tried to remove all sexist language and supplement existing worksheets with work designed more specifically for girls.

Collections of books suitable for class libraries have been examined systematically and where feasible many overtly sexist books have been thrown out. However, lack of suitable alternatives for all occasions has meant that overtly sexist books are still available. However, these where possible, have been relegated to the backs of the shelves and are not actively recommended by many teachers. All new purchases are, of course, selected very carefully.

Other strategies have included experimenting with single-sex groups for discussion purposes, where team teaching or extra support are available, and encouraging girls and boys to choose parts freely in play reading in class, particularly in a classic text where the 'best' parts are male.

Careers – Rowan

I receive an enormous amount of free careers literature, most of which is so sex-stereotyped that I refuse to use it. I have therfore had to devise the careers course material myself and have had difficulty using much of what is suggested in careers text books. This has meant extra work in changing pictures, sexes, wording etc. Fortunately, we have had an excellent Media Resources Officer who has been helpful in changing visual images.

The Careers department has also played a large role in the options system and I have persuaded subject teachers to give up some of their lesson time for me to talk about non-traditional career choices. I have also tried taking some single-sex careers lessons, which have been successful in stimulating girls to consider a wider range of career possibilities.

As a consequence, since the school formed links with three colleges for fifth-year courses some girls have shown an interest in doing the Motor Vehicle Link. I also recently organized a half-day conference for the third-year pupils on 'Equal Opportunities in Subject Choices', which was followed up by asking them to complete a questionnaire on their career intentions. Finally, women and men employed in areas not usually associated with their gender were invited to speak to the pupils.

In summary, it seems obvious to me that when talking to pupils their attitudes to careers are generally set in stereotyped ways. I believe that unless we can make more effort with pupils in their first three years of secondary school, they will continue in this way. A wider compulsory core of subjects in the fourth and fifth year would mean that both sexes would study a better balance of subjects and would consequently widen the choice of jobs open to them later. It is also vital to encourage parents to understand the limitations of sex-stereotyped attitudes since it is well known that young pupils can be very sensitive to family opinion.

Hidden Curriculum

Many of the changes made by the school have fallen within what is known as the 'hidden' or unofficial curriculum. In the main we have concentrated on trying to give greater support and strength to girls and women staff. Here we focus on a few of these changes.

Positive Action for Girls
Girls' club

A girls' club was started in September 1983 because it was felt that the majority of clubs run after school were dominated by boys. The club offers snooker, darts, table tennis, board games, dance, ice skating, and roller skating. In addition we intend to take the girls away for a weekend activity in the summer.

The main benefits which we believe have arisen from the girls' club have been:

1. Positive image reinforcement for the girls, basically just by the implication that girls are important enough to have their own club.
2. That it has given girls a forum and physical space in which to be active, vocal, strong or vulnerable without fear of criticism or anxiety about self-image.
3. That we have been able to encourage certain isolated and withdrawn girls to be involved. These girls have often benefited from being part of a girls'-only group and have often been surprised at their own abilities, whether at organizational tasks or, say, playing pool. Through informal chats and having fun with peers and staff they have become stronger and more confident.
4. That it has helped girls to form strong group bonds (in the past often the prerogative of boys) which have con-

tinued during school time.
5. That the club has given the girls opportunities to see female staff as active, fun-loving and also as vulnerable.

This has certainly improved our relationships with these girls during lesson time, and we feel that it has aided their learning potential.

Positive Action for Women Staff
Conferences
A half-day conference on equal opportunities for the whole staff was organized in school time. The acceptance of this conference by senior management gave the work of the equal opportunities group more credibility in the eyes of many teachers. This led to several weekend conferences, involving outside speakers. The details of our school policy and practices concerning both the hidden and overt curriculum were thus able to be constructed in a relaxed atmosphere.

The weekends have moreover allowed us, as women, to gain confidence and support from each other. This has been of great help back in school.

Courses
A weekend course on the use of computers was run for staff by the Head of Computer Studies. The majority of those who attended were women and the course resulted in a weekly after-school session for women teachers run by a female member of staff. This gave several women the knowledge and confidence to use computer programs as teaching aids. One was subsequently asked to make an 'expert' contribution to a course on the use of computers in Geography teaching.

Recommendations

Changes in certain parts of the curriculum have been patchy and have often been made by teachers with different ideas about the role of women within our society.

The girls' club and conferences have helped to reinforce the anti-sexist or feminist aspects of our work.

In changing the school curriculum we suggest the following:

1. that there should be institutionalized, regular monitoring by schools and the inspectorate
2. that teachers must be given time to work together to develop resources within their departments
3. that pressure needs to be put on examination boards to change both the syllabus and examinations, to ensure a non-sexist approach.

Conclusions

Over the last six years we feel we have achieved some success in giving confidence to girls and women staff, but we have still not succeeded in actively including parents and governors in our attempts to operate our school equal opportunities policy.

Certain departments have moved forward in changing curriculum and pedagogical practices. However, a changing ideological and economic climate makes our job more difficult. In our view, support must be given by the local authority in order to legitimate and give status to the actions of concerned teachers within schools. There is a constant need to remind people of why and how women are oppressed – in other words, to reaffirm basic feminist principles. Support from the hierarchy within our school and the local authority have been very useful in legitimizing our efforts.

In order to reconsider our original attitudes and approaches concerning women's oppression we have now, once more, formed a women's group to provide ourselves with a sense of direction and to give strength and support to ourselves as women and girl students. This is especially important at a time when there are fewer jobs available and women are being encouraged increasingly, particularly by the Media, to see themselves mainly as wives and mothers.

However, we still have an equal opportunities committee to spread our ideas more widely. Thus a 'marriage' has been forged between the 'anti-sexist' and 'equal opportunities' approaches which has resulted in strong areas of agreement about certain issues, ie. the need to remove blatant examples of sexism from our resources and curriculum. A greater number of women are now aware of male dominance and oppression. However, the question of 'what should we do about the boys?' still leads to different responses and is a question which still needs much further discussion.

CHAPTER 11

'Look, Jane, Look': Anti-sexist initiatives in primary schools.

ANTI-SEXIST WORKING PARTY*

Early experiences of sexism

Challenging the issues of sexism in primary schools is of crucial importance, especially when we consider that the early experiences of a child's life can be vital in determining her or his later attitudes and expectations. Before considering what schools can do we would like to briefly outline the factors which contribute to sexism in schools.

Children are born into a sexist society where women do not have equal opportunities and girls and boys have different experiences and expectations of themselves which are formed by society's attitudes as to what is appropriate for girls and boys to do.

These attitudes lead to male and female stereotyping. There is strong pressure on both sexes to conform to these stereotypes, even if this leads to conflict in their own lives.

---

* This article was written collectively by the women of the Anti-sexist Working Party:– Fiona Norman, Sue Turner, Jackie Granados Johnson, Helen Schwarcz, Helen Green, Jill Harris.

The female stereotype holds that girls and women are passive, nurturant, emotional and impractical. The characteristics of the male stereotype are activity, aggression, dominance and technical proficiency.

Before children come to school there are many examples of areas where conditioning and stereotyping exists. Girls and boys are dressed differently from birth, the emphasis for girls being on 'the pretty little girl in pink'. Girls are often dressed more impractically than boys which not only inhibits their choice of activities but carries the implicit message that certain activities are not suitable for girls.

Girls and boys are encouraged to play with different toys. By giving girls, and not boys, dolls to play with we reinforce the attitude that the caring role is the province of women, and at the same time we are, by implication, excluding men from this caring role. Approval is given to boys' games which involve physical activity, dominance and aggression, whereas similar behaviour in girls is unacceptable. Moreover, boys are encouraged to play with constructional toys which facilitate the development of mathematical and scientific concepts and this means that they have more experience and confidence in these areas than girls.

Girls and boys are differently reinforced and rewarded according to whether their behaviour is considered appropriate. Children therefore conform to the stereotypes presented. This conditioning and sex stereotyping comes both from within the home and outside. The media plays a large role in conditioning as children are constantly exposed to sexism in comics, books, TV programmes and advertising.

Inequalities in the primary school

By the time children come to school, they have already acquired a set of attitudes and expectations about what girls and boys can do. Primary schools need to challenge these attitudes rather than, as in the past, condone them. Girls tend to be academically more successful in primary schools but boys continue to learn that they have power and control.

So what are the primary schools doing in this area? The structure and organization of the majority of primary schools encourages girls and boys to be treated differently. This may range from grouping girls and boys separately on the register to sex-segregation in curricular activities such as games. Many books and resources used are sexist in content and illustration, thus reinforcing sex stereotypes. Boys monopolize/dominate certain classroom activities, such as constructional toys like Lego, and unless teachers intervene, girls get little opportunity to develop skills in these areas. Boys also dominate the physical space of the classroom and, from our own experience, dominate the teacher's time too so that girls have less opportunity to assert themselves and their learning.

Teachers often have different expectations of girls' and boys' behaviour and achievement, and these are highly influential, we believe, in challenging (and upholding) the assumed innate differences between the sexes. The language teachers use, both verbal and non-verbal, is important in creating a non-sexist environment.

So given that currently inequality of opportunity for girls and boys exists, we need to begin to think more critically about ways of challenging our own stereotyped attitudes and bring anti-sexist teaching strategies into the classroom. This we hope, will enable children to think for themselves, choose for themselves, and seek alternatives.

The Anti-sexist Working Party

The Anti-sexist Working Party is a group of classroom teachers working in a variety of inner city schools.

It was formed in 1981 at the DASI (Developing Anti-sexist Innovations) Conference for secondary teachers, which a number of 'isolated' primary teachers attended (Cornbleet & Sanders, 1982). Although previous projects had offered support to anti-sexist initiatives in secondary education, we could find no similar agency of support for primary teachers. Consequently we were isolated in our attempts to challenge the sexism we recognized in both the organization and curriculum of our schools.

We arranged to meet as a group and began to share the problems we faced in our own classrooms, identifying common experiences of discrimination against girls in our own schooling, which we saw clearly reflected in primary education today. We had all found it difficult to share with colleagues and parents our growing concern for these issues. We particularly wanted practical ideas for offering girls real equality through our own teaching. Working collectively we have tried out class projects, deliberately chosen to raise and challenge the issue of sexism; for instance, asking children to consider specific issues like 'Women and Work', 'Caring for Babies' and 'Girls and Sport'. Together we began to realize the need for positive images to support both girls and boys in questioning stereotypes. The ideas emerging from these projects form the basis of an exhibition we have developed to display the work of primary school children.

We have also examined areas of 'hidden' sexism and have tried to devise strategies for dealing with them. In particular, we have valued the effectiveness of working as a group to support our own optimism against a climate of hostility, and have recognized the importance of valuing and sharing personal classroom experience as crucial to in-service training.

We believe strongly that anti-sexist teaching strategies need to influence the curriculum and challenge the dynamics of the classroom. In general the domination of boys and passivity of girls creates a sexist environment where boys take more teacher time and aggressively pursue their own interests at the expense of girls.

Anti-sexist topics

In adopting an anti-sexist approach to teaching, the first
topic we chose to raise the relevant issues was 'Mums'.
Initial discussion, writing and artwork revealed the children's attitudes as already very stereotyped. For example,
we found in an infant class that 'mums' were drawn holding a broom by most of the children. When we questioned
the children about this we discovered that their mothers
actually used vacuum-cleaners but the school reading
scheme book presented this rather dated 'broom' image. In
this situation part of our approach was to help children to
acknowledge reality. We asked them 'What does your
Mum do?' Shopping, cleaning and working were the frequent responses. Further discussion broadened the list to
include painting, wallpapering, driving and 'fixing'
things. Such discussion raised the children's awareness of
the discrepancy between their own real experiences and
the stereotyped images they had met. They then went on to
make books to illustrate the statement 'My Mum is brave/
clever/strong' etc. This work on mothers was then
extended to other areas of the curriculum e.g. surveys of
jobs and leisure time, interviews with mothers about their
own childhood. Many of the children's mothers went out to
work, and looking at the jobs they did was important in
showing women's contribution to society. We arranged
talks and visits by mothers who were doing non-
stereotyped jobs and hobbies, which helped to expand the
children's views of women.

Creating time for class and group discussion where children feel able to explore, discuss and challenge sexism is
vital since we as female teachers often feel uncomfortable
when children express ideas like 'Mums should do all the
washing' and it can be tempting to say this is wrong, or to
imply it. In our experience the children will soon learn to
respond in a way that will win the teacher's approval. We
do not aim, however, to 'convert' children to think as we

do, but to offer them the space to think for themselves. We have found that children have a strong sense of fairness and justice and when given encouragement to make their own decisions are quick to challenge inequality. Once we had covered several themes in this way with our classes we felt that we had enough experience to approach most topics in an anti-sexist way. Examples included 'Space', 'Building' and 'Strength.'

When first introducing a topic we recognize that girls and boys bring different experiences and have different expectations of themselves. The enthusiasm and confidence with which boys will approach a topic like electricity will leave girls feeling uncertain and reluctant. We therefore feel that positive discrimination is necessary, and that girls need space, time and encouragement to become involved in design/technology, and science-based topics. Encouragement gives them a chance to participate equally with confidence. Another example of the need for positive discrimination is when mixed football is introduced. Girls will need time separate from boys to learn skills, and to feel confident and assertive in their use of space.

Giving girls space

Giving girls space is something the group believes is very important. In one of our schools some teachers expressed concern that 10 and 11 year-old boys dominated both classroom discussion and space in the playground. This led to an exploration of ways in which girls could be helped to become more assertive. It was decided to adopt an approach of positive intervention whence girls would be given time and space to think about the issues facing them. A room between two classes became 'the girls' room'. Meetings were held on a weekly basis with discussion as central to each session. The girls expressed their approval.

Anna: 'I like Tuesday mornings because it gives me a chance to speak about my true feelings. When the boys are around I feel embarrassed because I know the boys will laugh, but when I talk to girls they will share and understand my problem'.

The girls explored their feelings about being girls through drama, art, written work, and also by looking at the way the media presents the images of girls and women in advertisements and features. We then encouraged them to construct their own images of girls and women. They also have had the opportunity to work with tools and have made shelves for storing supplies of art paper.

> Cheryl: 'It was really good doing the shelves. Jill and Ayse helped me and at first it seemed hard, but after, when you pay attention to it, it gets really easy. I think it was good that it was just girls because boys always say "I'll do the good things, you go and pass me the things" '.

Initially the boys took little notice of what the girls were doing and it was only when the computer was introduced to the girls' room that they began to voice their objections. Plays that the girls presented at assembly time made the boys very defensive about the criticism they were hearing. A formal debate was held at which the motion that 'girls and boys in this school can work co-operatively' was carried. Since then the boys have been discussing why there is a girls' room, and have carried out their own research to find out if girls or boys receive more teacher time and if reading books and comics present biased images.

The girls have begun a project on women in history and are hoping to get a magazine printed. We suggest that a better deal for girls doesn't necessarily mean a worse deal for boys – it will probably just be different.

Having positive images such as posters and photos around the school is important, as is the way staff and helpers work together. There needs to be greater flexibility in using staff to challenge the hierarchical structure of schools. Examples such as a male teacher working with nursery or infant children can do much to encourage boys throughout the school to see caring for younger children as having value. In the same way it is important when women are confident and seem to be getting enjoyment from playing football and working with tools etc. This gives girls and boys a positive image with which to identify.

Language, books, drama

We try to avoid sexist language ourselves and encourage awareness of this amongst all school workers. By sexist language, we mean asking for strong boys to move furniture, comments on appearance confined to girls, statements like 'Early Man' or 'When Man invented the wheel'.

In class discussions we try to develop strategies for encouraging girls to participate e.g. the conch-shell game, in which only the person holding the shell can speak.

The stories we read to our classes are carefully chosen to avoid, as far as possible, stereotypes of race, class or sex. The children are encouraged to be critical of the books and comics they read, and to examine how and why they are sexist/racist, and what effect this may have. One way we do this is by working with reading schemes. Children have been encouraged to analyse the early books in the 'Sparks' scheme, looking at how females and males are portrayed and what activities they are doing. As well as re-writing many books in their own words, this has also lead to children re-drawing the illustrations and producing 'role-appearance' graphs. Children are also asked to look at books to see what they tell us about, how girls and boys are expected to be as adults. We try to extend this work by asking the children to make alternative versions of reading books. For instance, our version of the 'Dominoes' reading book, 'Things we do at school' shows girls and boys in a wide variety of activities both traditional and non-traditional. These activities and other alternative books made by the children have led to discussions about what actually happens in the classroom. Books that don't conform to

sexist-stereotypes for instance 'All the King's Horses' and
'The Paper Bag Princess' are used as a basis for discussion
and creative writing.

Drama need not be traditionally organized with a few
speaking parts and an audience. Everyone can be involved
and thus can then make alternative options more real for
children e.g. as part of a topic on 'Space', children were
encouraged to act out the discovery of a new planet where
the decision-makers were women. (See James, R. 1967,
Infant Drama, Nelson). Children can also be encouraged to
take on non-traditional roles as a way of helping them
explore sex-stereotypes and challenge assumptions about
sex differences. (Whyte, J. 1983; Joyce, K. 1983)

For younger children drama based on kinds of work will
help them talk about who does certain jobs and why.

The home corner is a space provided for children's own
private drama and regrettably often fails both to reflect the
diversity and wealth of the children's own cultures and to
acknowledge the changing role of women. Stereotyped
play is usually encouraged by the toys, and props that are
available in the home corner e.g. female dolls, pretty dressing-up clothes, kitchen furniture and utensils. Perhaps
the play would be less stereotyped and limited if we were
to provide a wider range of materials to reflect a broader
choice of adult roles e.g. various clothes for both sexes,
tools, games, male dolls. The home corner would then
become a place where children could explore different
adult roles.

> For all our futures, it will be just as important to have men
> who can be sensitive and caring as to have women who can
> be independent, confident and competent.
>
> Judith Whyte 'Beyond the Wendy House'.
> Longman for Schools Council, 1983.

Sharing and developing our ideas

As we mentioned earlier, we have assembled an exhibition

of the anti-sexist work currently being undertaken in our classrooms. This exhibition was produced as support material to help our own anti-sexist work and to disseminate our ideas as widely as possible to schools, teachers' centres and in the community. It was also a response to the questions teachers were asking, such as 'How do I start?'

We feel that classroom teachers most want practical ideas for classroom use, and the exhibition offers them ideas to try out so that they may consider their own anti-sexist approaches. We believe that by exposing children to a wide range of perspectives we can help them to move away from stereotypes and encourage a critical awareness and understanding of the issues.

How then does the group see its work developing? We are anxious to extend our resources, both to meet our own need for positive images in the classroom and to support colleagues in developing anti-sexist teaching strategies. The exhibition is on almost continuous loan throughout London and would seem to be one of the few visual displays of children's work available on the theme of anti-sexism. We have therefore decided that the making of a tape/slide programme to show this work is one of our priorities. This would ease the demand on the exhibition itself and enable our ideas to reach a wider audience. We are also in the process of investigating the possibilities of making a video, and assembling a collection of anti-sexist, anti-racist children's books, which could also be loaned out.

The group wishes to continue to provide support for teachers interested in forming their own anti-sexist groups, as well as contributing to the dissemination of ideas through in-service training. We are very aware of the need to reach a wider audience and would like to take the exhibition and ideas into the community to a greater extent than before perhaps displaying our exhibition in libraries and community centres. We need to consider ways of developing our relationships with parents and how to explain what we are trying to do, both to avoid conflicts and misunderstanding, and to gain their support.

Other issues we wish to consider more deeply are the links between sexism, racism and class-prejudice. These will include identifying ways in which schools can critically evaluate their perspectives and practice and thus raise their consciousness so that they are in a position to challenge the oppression inherent in the education system. As classroom teachers, we want to continue developing our own materials and strategies but at the same time act as a pressure group on education authorities, and other agencies so that they themselves develop non-sexist resources and make anti-sexist policy changes.

No matter how great the number of strategies we have and the breadth of resources or the support we give each other, we continually come up against the sexism 'hidden' in the structure of the system. For while teachers may be trying within the curriculum, to provide images for girls, the schools' own 'role-models' reinforce stereotypes. For example, in ILEA, one of the authorities which is actually trying to champion the cause of equal opportunities 80% of Primary School Teachers are women, 90% of Scale I teachers (the lowest scale) are women and yet only 54% of headteachers are women. Almost all the non-teaching staff in schools are female, with low status and pay, except for the school caretaker who is in a position of authority (all those keys!) and who is, almost without exception – male (ILEA, 1982).

There appears to be a contradiction in an LEA's equal opportunities programme which does not include consideration of an education authority's practice as an employer as well as the practical implementation of equal opportunities in the classroom. Lack of crèches for after-school courses, inadequate maternity leave and paid leave to tend sick children and almost non-existent paternity leave all serve to sustain inequality.

As a group we are realistic in our expectations and are not so naive as to think we can change the attitudes of society or the system over night. Nevertheless by offering children alternative images, and giving them the tools to critically examine the images they are surrounded by, we can at least make the issues visible.

It is crucial that school hierarchies support initiatives such as ours, because, unfortunately, children do not read authority guidelines and recommendations. They believe the evidence of their own eyes and their eyes tell them that power and authority still lies with the men.

We want to make education accessible to girls, not girls accessible to the education system.

CHAPTER 12

'Only Cissies Wear Dresses': A look at sexist talk in the nursery

NAIMA BROWNE & PAULINE FRANCE

It is a widely held belief in most nurseries that girls and boys are given similar opportunities to learn and develop and that they are not slotted into readily identifiable stereotypes. The sad reality is that sexism *does* occur in most nursery classrooms – largely because such establishments tend to uphold this society's perceived norms of behaviour and so help to perpetuate the sexist stereotyping and discriminatory practices children experience from birth.

Sexism and stereotyping in the nursery are generally not deliberate – most staff are sincere in their wish to give equal support to girls and boys in their care. But even the most caring and sensitive of adults can, at times, reinforce traditional stereotypes of what women and men, girls and boys are like and can do.

We intend to discuss some of the ways we have noticed sexism operating in our experience as teachers in multilingual nurseries around inner and East London. The examples we have used come from classroom observations, tape and video recordings and also from a month of closely monitoring ourselves and reflecting on the way we talk to and behave with children. The main focus of this article will be on language and how it is used to regulate children's behaviour, and transmit a socially acceptable view of the world.

As teachers working in multilingual classrooms we feel it is crucial to start with a close examination of the language we use to help children build up a picture of this multicultural society. It is equally important to consider the influences exerted by our actions and the visual images we present to the children. Yet within the scope of this article we cannot hope to cover these two areas extensively and we have chosen simply to indicate some very practical steps we have taken to inform ourselves and our colleagues in developing an anti-sexist nursery policy.

'Language uses us as much as we use language'
(Robin Lakoff, 1975)

Examining the way we talk to young children can be a revealing practice. We learn about our perceptions of people in this society and our expectations of girls' and boys' behaviour and achievements. Not only do young children quite frequently witness sexist comments in their daily lives but they are also encouraged to use language in sexually stereotyped ways.

Sexist talk begins when a child is born, so that by the time she is ready to come to school she is well versed in the ways of thinking and talking that will enable her to fit quite happily into our sexist society. (Belotti, 1975. Greenberg, 1978. Bean, 1978)

From a child's earliest experiences of talk she will be learning how to label, name and make references to herself and others. Research into 'baby talk' (or the sexist term 'motherese') highlights the unusually high amount of naming and labelling that goes on in the adults' speech to a baby. (Ferguson & Snow, 1977). For example instead of saying 'I'll do it' the adult is more likely to say 'Mum/Dad will do it'. Similarly the instruction 'Do it' or 'You do it' will include reference to the baby or child being instructed, as in 'Kiran do it'. This naming activity is an important aspect of socialization – the child learns her name, a significant marker of her identity and her relationship with others. As horizons broaden so a child needs additional terms of reference – further terms for herself, close relatives and the ever growing number of people, young and old, she will meet.

In monitoring our own speech with young children, as well as that of colleagues in multilingual nurseries we became aware that not all of the most commonly used terms of reference are applied equally to girls and boys. More alarmingly, we noted some terms used exclusively with girls have negative connotations.

Labels that emphasise the adult's authority and the child's dependence draw heavily on diminutive descriptions. We found these cropped up most frequently in conversations with girls: adults called them 'little one', 'little miss', 'little girl', or even 'little thing'. Only very young and tiny boys were called 'little one'. The term 'little boy' seemed to be used in a slightly sardonic way, with the boy so addressed being drawn into the joke, 'little mister' which could be seen as an equivalent of 'little miss' never appeared. It is interesting that the term 'little man' is quite common in the speech of many parents and grandparents when addressing a young male baby. This is generally replaced by 'young man' as the child moves out of his first or second year.

We found that 'little' was rarely far away from our lips when we referred to older girls and images of women. So when sharing books, playing with toy people and dolls, painting and drawing we frequently juxtaposed 'Here's the man/boy' with 'and there's the little woman/girl'. So it seems that boys are allowed to grow up much more quickly than girls and are made aware from the start that they will become men. Girls are kept small and controllable. 'Miss' the one term used with young girls which could be said to point forward to adulthood is unfortunate as it makes reference to a woman's marital status, so defining a woman in terms of her relationship to a man.

Whilst 'young man' was used with nursery aged boys, as a measure of reproof, the equivalent for girls was not 'young woman' but 'young lady'. This leads us into an interesting yet controversial area of English language usage. Children are taught to use the word 'lady' because, so the belief goes, it is 'politer' than 'woman'. This insistence on politeness about and to women makes a whole host of assumptions about the status of women in our society. How have we let our language develop to the stage that being called a woman is not nice – presumably because *being* a woman is not nice? Why must a polite euphemism be found? The insult to women is further compounded if we consider that 'woman' is somehow on a par with other terms needing euphemisms – words like 'toilet', 'dead', 'copulating' and so on.

So girls learn from an early age that it is not nice to be merely a 'woman' – we have to aspire to be 'ladies' instead. Ladies act in certain socially conditioned ways – they have manners, don't use certain words, don't get their clothes dirty or eat messily, and of course they never wear trousers, lift heavy objects, climb fences . . . the list is endless. The reproof 'young lady' serves as a reminder of all of this in a way that cannot be paralleled by 'young man'. Why should women need politer treatment than men? Should we not be encouraging a caring and considerate attitude to *all* people in the children in our charge? By expecting consideration women signal a degree of helplessness and fragility which only serves to bolster up men's feeling of power and authority.

An extension of this can be found in job terminology. We found a common feature of talk about working people with young children was that job names, which could be sexually neutral were assumed to refer only to men. So when a reference was made to a doctor, driver, pilot, manager etc. and the sex of that person was unspecified, the pronouns 'he', 'him', and 'his' were employed. This usage gives a distorted picture of real life – for it is now the experience of many of our children that women can be managers, doctors, drivers and so on. Ironically and sadly, we have found that daughters of anti-sexist parents have learnt from this sexist use of language and are likely to assert that women cannot be doctors. This forces us into the insulting position of coining female versions, such as 'woman doctor', 'woman driver' . . . . A further insult comes from the practice of replacing 'woman' by 'lady', which also tends to trivialize the serious achievements of the woman concerned.

Thus we cover up the demeaning nature of much of women's work by using the term 'lady' e.g. 'dinner lady', 'cleaning lady', 'sales lady', 'lollipop lady'. These cosy euphemisms mask the tedious yet strenuous nature of such work and moreover state categorically that it is 'woman's work'.

Gender-related labelling or naming also applied to nicknames. Girls were bombarded with terms of endearment – 'honey', 'sweetie', 'lovey', 'darling', 'treasure', 'precious', 'little charmer' . . . whereas boys got terms that reinforce the tough macho behaviour expected of them – 'buster', 'bruiser', 'toughie', 'big bully', 'wise guy' and so on. The act of nicknaming is a subtle way of defining power relations between adults and children. Although nicknames can reveal a degree of closeness and warmth from the adult user to the child, they also help to establish the adult's authority and control over the child. The decision to adapt a name or use any sort of nickname rests solely with the adult. Young children are never allowed to return the 'compliment'. We have only ever witnessed children using nicknames to toys or as part of their role play and storytelling.

It is comforting for children to receive terms of endearment when they are sincerely meant. In our experience these terms are hardly ever offered to older boys in the nursery – for some reason it is 'unmanly' for them to be given signs of warmth and affection. Terms expressing toughness are used to a boy from his earliest days – we know of a four-month old boy who was persistently called 'buster' by his grandparents, despite his parents' objections. Terms of endearment can be used indiscriminately, and some would say patronizingly, to girls and often remain with them for life. Many women find it insulting to be called 'dear' by a man they hardly know.

Some girls do get tough sounding nicknames, like 'butch' – but only in cases where those girls reveal qualities normally associated with boys. Girls who are confident, outward going, assertive and physically active are called 'tomboys' and this is used as a term of approval – as long as they recognize their limitations as girls. Girls have already learnt this message by the time they come to the nursery. In one class a Bengali-speaking girl told the staff she was changing her name from Nigat to Tony, because 'boys have all the fun'. She refused to wear dresses and play only with girls. Fortunately for her she had a teacher and parents who did not feel threatened or distressed by her rejection of all things feminine. They encouraged her assertiveness and at the same time helped her to become more positive about being a girl. Not all girls find the same support though. It is generally more widely acceptable for a young girl strongly to identify with boys than for a boy to enjoy girls company, and behave in any way that could be called girlish. 'Tomboy' certainly has none of the stigma that is attached to the word 'cissy'. In our classroom observations and recording we found that 'cissy' was used by adults to or about some boys and also between children. It was always used as an insult – the message being that to act or appear like a girl is a sign of weakness. Many adults are desperate to suppress any identification with girls by young boys.

In our work in schools we frequently encountered the phrases 'proper little madam' or 'right little madam' used as a put down of any girl who showed any signs of individuality, confidence or assertiveness – qualities applauded when they appear in boys. In fact we could not find a similarly critical description that could be applied to a boy. 'Proper little gent' is used generally as a term of approval to refer to a boy who is careful about his appearance, manner and behaviour – qualities expected to happen naturally in girls.

The descriptive terms 'daddy's girl' and 'mummy's boy' continue this positive/negative dichotomy. To be a 'daddy's girl' is not only socially acceptable but also highly desirable as it places a girl firmly under the influence and control of a man right from the start. To be a 'mummy's boy' is very definitely negative. In fact it has been attributed as the root cause of sexual deviance in later life. This insulting use of an ostensibly harmless phrase highlights the sexism rampant in our society. Women are the losers on all counts: they are expected to be care-givers looking after children with love and affection. Yet when such care is warmly reciprocated by a male child women are blamed for sowing the seeds of sexual problems.

Some descriptive terms used frequently with young children clearly define the type of behaviour and characteristics deemed acceptable in girls yet unacceptable in boys, or vice versa. We give some common examples of this in Table 1.

Some terms are clearly sex-specific and have no counterpart when used for the other sex. We have noticed constant pressure on boys to be 'tough', 'brave', 'big and strong' – all in all 'a real boy'. Girls gain social approval from being 'sweet natured', 'neat and tidy', 'docile', at times a 'busy bee' yet at all times 'pretty and domesticated'.

Our obsession with attractive physical appearance in girls crops up in conversations between adults and children in the nursery. From our tape recordings we have noticed that a common opening gambit made by adults to girls concerned the clothes they were wearing, for example:

'You've got new shoes on. They're a nice colour.'
'That's a pretty dress. You haven't worn that before.'

TABLE 1   *Sex-specific descriptive terms commonly found in conversation with or about children in the nursery.*

Qualities or behaviour (neutral descriptions)	Description if girl	Description if boy
1) Quiet and withdrawn, diffident with adults	Shy	Strong silent type
2) Noisy, rushing rapidly around from one activity to another	Disturbed, disruptive, over excited	Boisterous, lively, active
3) Showing emotions freely, crying particularly if upset	Sensitive	Wet, big softie, cry-baby
4) Quiet but obviously unhappy	Sulkypuss, crosspatch	Angry, hurt
5) Organizing others, initiating activities	Bossy	Born leader
6) Trying to do something despite difficulties	Stubborn	Determined
Physical Characteristics		
1) Slim, slender, below average weight	Delicate	Skinny, weedy
2) Above average weight	Fat, plump	Stocky, well-built, solid
3) Attractive	Beautiful, pretty	Good-looking, handsome
4) Having a 'winning smile' and 'twinkle in the eye'	Cute, sweet	Cheeky faced
5) Calling loudly and high pitched	Shrieking, screaming	Shouting, yelling
6) Complaining angrily about something, voice trembling, close to tears	Whinging, whining	Grumbling, moaning

'That ribbon matches the red in your dress.'

Conversations about clothes with boys tended towards more practical aspects, for example:

'Those shoes look comfortable.'
'I bet those shoes are good for splashing in puddles.'
'Those trousers feel warm.'

Girls are complimented on their appearance, whilst boys are frequently reproached for getting messy. Of course it is always suggested that where necessary their mothers will have to do the washing.

In fact we found that adults revealed very stereotyped expectations of mothers' and fathers' roles in their conversations with young children. Women tend to be talked about in terms of home-based roles and relationships to men, 'shopkeeper's wife', 'boy's mummy' and so on. Men are presented in a diversity of jobs and professions. We find this very disturbing as it fails to broaden children's experience of different life styles and does not in fact reflect the reality of inner city life.

In London many households are run and financed by parents who both work and share household chores. But there are also homes where unemployment and/or single parenthood go against conventional stereotypes. Cultural and racial stereotypes also complicate the issue. A lack of real understanding of other cultures has led nursery staff to develop a simplistic view of different life styles, full of over-generalizations and stereotyped notions of 'accepted' norms of behaviour in those cultures. So it is frequently asserted that children of Caribbean parents experience a rigid discipline at home and the boys find it difficult to cope with the relative freedom at school. Similarly it is believed that boys from 'patriarchal' cultures e.g. Greek, Middle Eastern, Cypriot, Muslim, have a low regard for women and so will not respect women teachers. Expectations of parents are equally stereotyped. Muslim fathers are characterized as more sexist and oppressive than other fathers and are frequently cited as presenting a barrier to anti-sexist initiatives in the nursery.

From our experience of dealing with fathers from a diversity of cultural backgrounds we feel it is far too simplistic to attribute sexism to all men from a particular ethnic group and prefer to deal with people as individuals. In one class for instance the teacher organized an outing and encouraged parents to come along. Later she expressed disappointment and concern that, although one of the Muslim fathers had made a great effort to come and was in fact the only man there, he had given no active support all day and seemed only to have come 'to keep an eye on his wife'. By dismissing this as an example of sexism in Muslim men the teacher failed to take account of several important points, such as the guidance we give to parents, and particularly fathers, on how they can help; the relationship between individual parents involved in such an outing; and the expectations of other parents towards a solitary male.

We recognize that nursery staff have a very demanding job in developing and putting into practice an anti-sexist approach to early learning. By adopting as they do an 'open door' policy to their class they accept the fact that other adults can play a role in the education of the children in their charge. On the whole staff have stressed the important and valuable contribution made by parents, older children, students, workers in the community and the like and frequently encourage visits from these people to the class. It is, however, necessary to be aware of the potentially damaging influences that can also be exerted, unless visitors are helped to understand the nursery policy and practice particularly on issues of anti-racism and anti-sexism.

Just how hurtful a casual comment can be is clearly illustrated by this incident. A class of 25 children included four boys. All the boys had been encouraged to play with and make the most out of the home corner and dressing-up resources. One boy particularly enjoyed putting on a dress, hat, veil, and beads and often kept this outfit on whilst engaged in other play. However, one day the boy's involvement in quite an extended and creative fantasy was spoilt by an unthinking comment. The local milkman who generally brought in milk to the class each day always stopped for a chat with one or two children. When he saw the boy wearing a dress he exclaimed 'What a pretty girl!' The boy protested that he was not a girl but was told abruptly that 'real boys don't wear dresses. Only cissies do.' The boy tore off the dress, trampled on it and refused to wear it again. Fortunately, as the teacher was nearby she was able to talk this through in a friendly way with the milkman and also gradually help the boy to experiment with other dressing-up clothes.

This type of comment can be doubly hurtful – it hurts the child concerned because he is given signs of social rejection for something hitherto enjoyable: it hurts all the girls who may have overheard because it states categorically that appearing like a girl is considered wrong by a respected and popular adult. What must he think if you not only *appear* like one but actually *are* a girl!

Ultimately we cannot stop others from holding sexist beliefs and attitudes. What we can do is present many possible alternatives and so help our children to cope with difficult situations in which their actions and assumptions may be challenged.

Points to consider when working towards an anti-sexist policy in the nursery

The following list of suggestions is neither comprehensive nor finite but merely some practical steps we ourselves have found useful.

1) Monitor your own and your colleagues use of language. We found that recording and analysing the terms of

reference, labels and descriptive phrases most commonly used as well as the content of conversations we had with girls and boys, enabled us to make conscious effort to avoid using language in a way liable to perpetuate sexist attitudes.

2) Review the stories and songs used in your nursery.

Careful examination may expose a predominance of dynamic, active, problem solving male characters on hand to rescue or marry the weak, domesticated, pretty, passive female. (e.g. it is a boy who goes exploring in 'Where the Wild Things Are' and a male doctor who provides the cure in the song 'Miss Polly had a Dolly'). Useful strategies to help minimize sexism in stories and songs include retelling and adapting the text so that it is often the girls and women who are competent and adventurous and the boys and men who provide care or are in need of reassurance themselves. (e.g. enable the mother to solve the problems in 'The Tiger who came to Tea' and when telling stories that explore emotions have boys as well as girls who feel upset or are afraid of the dark). Similarly, where the main character is an animal simply change 'he' to 'she' (e.g. the 'Five Little Monkeys Bouncing on the Bed' need not be male, neither does the puppy in the various 'Spot' books).

3) Monitor your own behaviour towards children and your reactions to the children's behaviour.

Once any differences in our behaviour towards girls and boys become exposed and any gender and race related differences in expectations of 'acceptable' behaviour is highlighted, it is possible to develop strategies whereby *all* children in the nursery are encouraged to be caring and considerate as well as self-confident enough to explore and experiment. Simple steps that can help achieve this include choosing boys to care for new children, encouraging girls to be physically adventurous and to solve problems unaided and enabling boys to express their emotions particularly when hurt or upset.

4) Observe the children's choice of activity.

   It is common for sex-specific 'territories' to be infor-
   mally defined in some nurseries (e.g. girls will be found
   in the home corner and participating in quieter
   activities, boys will be in the brick corner, playing with
   cars or outside on big toys). If the teacher is aware of a
   similar situation in his/her nursery it is possible to
   encourage both sexes to venture into other 'territories'
   by making a deliberate effort on the adult's part to participate equally in all the activities.

5) Review the visual images presented to all the children.

   When we carried out a systematic review of the visual
   images which surround children in their nursery, we
   were surprised to discover how pervasive sexism was in
   resources produced specifically for educational purposes. For a comprehensive review you will need to
   analyse all the posters, pictures, puzzles, games, card
   games, coat-peg labels, books, magazines, newpapers,
   catalogues and furnishings available in the nursery.
   Obviously we have to use what is on offer but the effect
   of sexist images can be diminished by talking to children about sexual and racial stereotyping and suggesting
   alternatives.

6) Critically examine your use of human resources.

   When inviting visitors to the nursery try to choose individuals who will not reinforce sexist attitudes and will
   be willing to engage in non-stereotyped activities (e.g.
   have a father bathing a baby or a woman trumpet-
   player).

7) Produce an anti-sexist policy statement and guidelines
   in multilingual versions and talk to the parents about
   this.

   If the policy is both prominently displayed and distributed to all parents and visitors, it will help to minimize
   problems arising through misunderstandings. By talking together, parents and nursery workers are likely to
   increase their understanding of each other's views,
   attitudes and expectations.

8) Tackle sexism wherever it occurs.
Sexism, like racism, is pernicious, irrational and hurtful and instances should be dealt with as they occur. Failing to face the issue implies tacit agreement.

REFERENCES

Ardener, S., (ed.), (1981). *Women and Space*. Croom Helm.

Banks, O. (1981). *Faces of Feminism*. Martin Robertson.

Barrett, M. (1980). *Women's Oppression Today*, NLB.

Barry, K. (1981). *Female Sexual Slavery*. Aron Books, NY.

Bean. J., (1978). 'The Development of Psychological Androgeny: Early Childhood Socialisation' in *Perspectives on Non-Sexist Childhood Education*, Spring, B., (ed.) Teachers' College Press.

Beecham, Y. (1983). 'Women's Studies and Beyond – The Feminisation of Education', *Gen*. WedG, No. 1, Autumn.

Belotti, G. (1975). *Little Girls*, Writers and Readers Publishing Cooperative.

Bennett, Y. & Carter, D., (1981). *Sidetracked*, EOC.

Brah, A., (1979). *Inter-generational and inter-ethnic perceptions among Asian and White adolescents and their parents*, PhD thesis, Bristol University.

Brah, A., (1982). *Culture and Identity; the case of South Asians*, E 354, Block 3, Units 8–9, Open University.

Byrne, E., (1978). *Women and Education*, Tavistock.

Campbell, B., (1984a). 'How the Other Half Lives', *Marxism Today*, April.

Campbell, B., (1984b). *Wigan Pier Revisited; Poverty and Politics in the 80s*, Virago.

Carby, H., (1982). 'White Woman Listen! Black Feminism and the Boundaries of Sisterhood', *The Empire Strikes Back*, (ed.) CCCS, Hutchinson.

Centre for Contemporary Cultural Studies, (1981).*Unpopular Education*, Hutchinson.

C.C.C.S. (1982). *The Empire Strikes Back*. Hutchinson.

Clarke, L., (1980). *Occupational Choice; a critical review of research in the UK.*, D. of E., Careers Service Branch.

Cliffe, M., (1980). *Claiming an Identity They Taught me to Despise*, Persophone Press.

Cornbleet, A. & Sanders, S. (1982). *Developing Anti-sexist Initiatives (DASI); Project Report*, ILEA.

Cornbleet, A. & Libovitch, S. (1983). 'Anti-sexist Initiatives in a Mixed Comprehensive School; a case study', in *Is There Anyone Here From Education*, (eds.) Wolpe, A. & Donald, J., Pluto Press.

Coveney, L. *et al.* (1984). *The Sexuality Papers; Male Sexuality and the Social Control of Women*, Hutchinson.

Coventry County Council (1984). *Coventry Quarterly Monitor of the Local Economy 1/84*.

Davies, A., (1980). *Women, Race & Class*, Women's Press.

Department of Education and Science (1975). 1) *Curricular Differences for*

Boys and Girls; Education Survey 21, HMSO.

(1979) 2) *A Survey of Secondary Education; HMI Survey,* HMSO.

(1980) 3) *Girls and Science; HMI Matters for Discussion 13,* HMSO.

(1981) 4) *The School Curriculum,* HMSO.

Dworkin, A., (1981). *Pornography; Men Possessing Women.* The Women's Press.

Equal Opportunities Commission

(1979) reprinted 1983. *Do You Provide Equal Educational Opportunities?* EOC.

(1982) *EOC Research Bulletin,* No. 6, EOC Spring.

Ferguson, C. & Snow, C. (eds.) (1977). *Talking to Children,* C.U.P.

Feuchtwang, S.. (1980). 'Socialist, Feminist and Anti-racist Struggles' *Marxist Feminist,* No. 4.

Fogarty, M. *et al.* (1971). *Sex, Career and Family,* Allen & Unwin.

Foreman, M., (1976). *All the King's Horses,* Hamish Hamilton.

Fuller, M., (1980). 'Black Girls in a London Comprehensive School' in *Schooling for Women's Work,* (ed.) Deem, R., Routledge and Kegan Paul.

Fuller, M., (1983). 'Qualified Criticism, Critical Qualifications' in *Race, Class and Gender,* (eds.) Barton, L. & Walker, S. Falmer Press.

Fuller, M., (1984). Inequality; *Gender, Class and Race,* E205 Block 6 Unit 27, Open University.

Greenberg, S., (1978). *Right from the Start; a guide to non-sexist child-rearing,* Houghton & Mifflin.

Hall, S. *et al.* (1978). *Policing the Crisis,* Hutchinson.

HMSO *Interim Report; Rampton*

Hill, E., (1980). *Where's Spot* and *Spot's Birthday* Heinneman.

Hooks, B., (1981). *'Ain't I a Woman?';* *Black Women and Feminism,* Pluto Press.

Hull, Bell, Scott & Smith (eds.) (1982). *'But some of us are brave, all the women are white, all the blacks are men?;* Black Women's Studies, Feminist Press.

Inner London Education Authority

(1981). *Achievement in Schools: Sex Differences,* Report RS 806/81.

(1982). *Achievement in Schools* RS 829/82

(1982). *Equal Opportunities for Boys & Girls; A Report by the ILEA Inspectorate,* Autumn.

Jackson, M., (1983). Sexual Liberation or Social Control? Some Aspects of the Relationship between Feminism and the Social Construction of Sexual Knowledge in the Early Twentieth Century', *Women's Studies International Forum,* Pergamon Press.

James, R., (1967). *Infant Drama,* Nelson.

Jeffreys, S., (1982a). 'The Sexual Abuse of Children in the Home', in *The Problem of Men,* (eds.) Friedman, S. & Sarah, E., The Women's Press.

Jeffreys, S., (1982b). 'Free from all Uninvited Touch of Man; Women's Campaigns Around Sexuality 1880–1914, *Women's Studies International Forum,* Vol. 5, No. 6.

Jeffreys, S., (1983). 'Sex Reform and Anti-feminism in the 1920s', *The Sexual Dynamics of History*, London Feminist History Group, Pluto Press.

Jeffreys, S., (1985). *The Spinster and her Enemies; Feminism and Sexuality 1880–1930*, R & KP.

Jessop, B., (1982). *The Capitalist State; Marxists Theories and Methods* Martin Robertson.

John, G., (1981). *In the Service of Black Youth*, National Association of Youth Clubs.

Joyce, K., (1983). 'Sex-stereotyping through drama', quoted in *Beyond the Wendy House*, Whyte, J., Longman.

Kant, L. & Browne, M., (1984). *Jobs for the Girls*, Schools Council.

Kelly, A., (1981). *The Missing Half: Girls and Science Education*, Manchester University Press.

Kerr, J., (1972). *The Tiger Who Came to Tea*, Collins.

King, R., (1978). *All Things Bright and Beautiful*, Wiley.

Lakoff, R., (1975). *Language and a Woman's Place*, Harper & Row.

Lederer, L. (ed.) (1981). *Take Back the Night*, Marrow-Quill Paperbacks, NY.

Leech, K., (1983). 'From Small Beginnings; Multi-cultural work at Plumstead Manor – A personal view, *Multi-ethnic Education Review*, ILEA, Vol. 1, No. 2.

Little, A. & Wiley, R., (1981). *Multi-ethnic Education; The Way Forward*, Schools Council Pamphlet 18.

London Rape Crisis Centre (1984). *Sexual Violence – the Reality for Women*, The Women's Press.

Mahoney, P., (forthcoming) *Co-education for Boys*.

Millman, V., (1982). *Double Vision: the post-school experiences of 16–19 year-old girls*, Coventry LEA.

Millman, V., (1984a). 'Are Girls Getting a Raw Deal?', *Where*, ACE, Feb.

Millman, V., (1984b). *Teaching Technology to Girls; A Workshop Approach*, Coventry LEA.

Millman. V. & Weiner, G., (1984). *'Is there really a problem? Sex Differentiation in Schools*, Longman.

Minhas, R. (1982). *Institutionalised Racism*. MSc Dissertation, London University Institute of Education.

Mitchell, J., (1971). *Women's Estate*, Pelican.

Moraga, C. & Anzaldua, (eds.) (1981). *This Bridge Called My Back – writings by radical women of colour*, Persophone Press.

Munsch, R. N. (1980). *The Paper Bag Princess*, Hippo.

National Union of Teachers (1980). *Promotion and the Woman Teacher*, NUT.

Nelson, S., (1982). *Incest – Fact & Myth*, Stramullion, Edinburgh.

Newsom, J. (Chair) (1963). *Half Our Future; the Newsom Report*, HMSO.

OWAAD (1979). *Organisation of Women of Asian and African Descent, Conference Report*.

Parmar, P., (1982). 'Gender, race and class; Asian women in resistance',

Empire Strikes Back, (ed.) CCCS, Hutchinson.

Parmar, P. & Mirza, N., (1983). 'Stepping Forward – working with Asian young women' *Gen*, Issue 1, Autumn.

Rampton Report (June 1981) *Interim Report: West Indian Children in Our Schools*, HMSO.

Rapoport, R. & Rapoport, R. N., (1978). *Working Couples*, R & KP.

Raynor, R., (1984a). 'The Death of the Permissive Society', *Time Out*, March 1st.

Raynor, R., (1984b). 'The Sexual Backlash', *Time Out*, March 7th.

Rich, A., (1980). 'Taking Women's Studies Seriously, *On Lies, Secrets and Silence*, Virago.

Rubinstein, D., (1984). *Equal Educational Opportunity, the Tripartite System and the Comprehensive School*, E205, Block 2, Unit 6, Open University.

Rush, F., (1980). *The Best Kept Secret*, McGraw Hill, USA.

Sarah, E., (1982). 'Towards a Reassessment of Feminist History', editorial, *Women's Studies International Forum*, Vol. 5, No. 6.

Schools Council/ILEA, (1983). *Equal Opportunities; What's in it for Boys?* Conference Report.

Sendak, M., (1967). *Where the Wild Things Are*, Bodley Head.

Smith, S., (1984). Single-sex Setting, *Co-education Reconsidered*, (ed.) Deem, R., Open University Press.

Spare Rib, (1983). (uncredited) 'Sexual Harassment in Schools', *Spare Rib*, June.

Spender, D., (1978). *Times Educational Supplement*, November.

Spender, D., (1982a). *Invisible Women; The Schooling Scandal*, Writers & Readers Publishing Cooperative.

Spender, D., (1982b). *Women's Ideas and What Men Have Done to Them.* Ark Paperbacks.

Spender, D. & Sarah, E. (eds.) (1980). *Learning to Lose; Sexism and Education.* The Women's Press.

Stanworth, M., (1983). *Gender and Schooling; A Study of Sexual Divisions in the Classroom*, Hutchinson.

Sutherland, M., (1981). *Sex Bias in Education*, Blackwell.

Taylor, H., (1984). 'An Open Cupboard Policy', *Issues in Race and Education*, No. 41, Spring.

Times Educational Supplement, (1983a) 1) 'Protest over head's appointment', *TES*, frontpage, June 24.

(1983b) 2) Untitled, July 29.

(1984) 3) 'Study on exams finds Asians most positive', *TES*, 13 April.

Tomlinson, S., (1983). 'Black women in Higher Education – Case Studies of University Women in Britain', in Barton and Walker (eds), *Race, Class and Education*, Croom Helm.

Ward, E., (1984). *Father–Daughter Rape*, The Women's Press.

Walker, S. & Barton, L., (1983). *Gender, Class and Education*, Falmer Press.

Weiner, G., (1976). Girls' Education, the Curriculum and the Sex

Discrimination Act, London University Institute of Education MA Dissertation, Chap. 3.

Weiner, G., (1978). 'Education and the Sex Discrimination Act', *Educational Research,* NFER, 20 (3).

Whitbread, A., (1980). 'Female Teachers Are Women First – Sexual Harassment at Work', *Learning to Lose,* (eds.), Spender, D. & Sarah, E., The Women's Press.

Whylde, J. (ed.) (1983). *Sexism in the Secondary School Curriculum,* Harper & Row.

Whyte, J., (1983). *Beyond the Wendy House; Sex-role Stereotyping in Primary Schools,* Schools Council/EOC, Longman.

Wilce, H., (1984). 'Walking the tight-rope between two cultures', *TES,* 10 Feb.

Woolf, V., (1938). *Thirty Guineas,* The Hogarth Press.

Women Against Violence Against Women (WAVAW) (1982). 'Pornography', *Spare Rib,* No. 119, June.

Resources

Documents published by the Equal Opportunities Commission

Aspects of secondary education in England – a survey by HM Inspectors of schools: the EOC response, 1980.

Breakthrough – a pictorial record of 5 years' progress towards sex equality in employment, 1980.

Careers opportunities and education, Brown, M., 1981.

Committee of Inquiry into the teaching of mathematics: comment by the EOC, 1979.

Do you provide equal opportunities?: A guide to good practice in the provision of equal opportunities in education, 1979, 1983.

Education for girls: a statistical analysis, 1981.

Education in schools: a consultative document: the reponse of the EOC, 1977.

Ending sex stereotyping in schools, Hannon, V., 1981.

EOC comments on the DES report, Local authority arrangements for the school curriculum: report on the Circular 14/77 review, 1979.

Equal opportunities in education, 1975.

Getting It Right Matters – a guide for parents to subject options for their children, 1982.

Guidelines for the Secretary of State for the elimination of sex discrimination in schemes of secondary school education, 1979.

Guide to equal treatment of the sexes in careers materials, 1980.

Positive sex discrimination in training schemes, 1981.

Primary schools careers posters: notes for guidance, 1980.

Providing educational opportunities for 16–19 year olds: the EOC response, 1979.

Sidetracked! – a look at careers advice given to 5th form girls,
Bennett, Y. & Carter, D., 1981.
Wider Horizons, 1981.

Audio-visual Aids

Cinema of Women   *Taught to be Girls*
Unit 160   *Linda Beyond the Expected*
27 Clerkenwell Close   *Token Gesture*
London EC1R 0AT   *Who needs nurseries? We Do.*
                                        Give Us a Smile

EOC (Visual Aids)   *A Question of Attitudes*
Central Film Library   *What are you really made of?*
Chalfont Grove   *What's a girl like you?*
Gerrards Cross
Buckinghamshire SL9 8TN

Sheffield Film Co-op   *A Question of Choice*
34 Psalter Lane
Sheffield S11

Women in Manual Trades   *Building your Future*
Concord Film Council Ltd
201 Felixstowe Road
Ipswich
Suffolk IP3 9BJ

Contact Organizations

Advisory Centre for Education (ACE)
18 Victoria Park Square
London E29 PB (Tel. 01–928–9222)

Campaign Against Sexism and Sexual Oppression in
Education (CASSOE)
17 Lymington Road
London NW6 (Tel. 01–435–6189)
(Newsletter 6 times a year)

Equal Opportunities Commission (EOC)
Overseas House
Quay Street
Manchester M3 3HN

Regional Offices
Caerwys House
Windsor Lane
Cardiff CF1 1LB

149 West George Street
Glasgow G2 4QE

Incest Survivors Campaign (ISC)
c/o A Woman's Place
Hungerford House
Victoria Embankment
London WC2

Incest Survivors Campaign exists as a self-help group for girls and women who have been sexually abused which also campaigns against the sexual abuse of girls. Contact ISC at the following address. This is a c/o address and therefore ISC cannot be contacted by phone.

Letterbox Library
Children's Book Cooperative
1st floor, 5 Bradbury Street
London N16 8JN (Tel. 01–254–1640)
'A group of women committed to making non-sexist books for children more widely available'. £2.50 subscription – regular newsletter and list of titles.

National Advisory Centre on Careers for Women
Drayton House
30 Gordon Street
London WC1H 0AX

London Rape Crisis Centre
PO Box 69
London WC1X 9NJ (Tel. 01–837–1600)
Rape Crisis Centres have been set up around Britain. For the telephone number of your local centre and for the 24-hour counselling line of the London Rape Crisis Centre telephone the above number.

Rights of Women Unit
National Council for Civil Liberties
21 Tabard Street
London SE1 4LA

Sheffield Women in Education Group
c/o Margaret Anderson
99, Psalter Avenue, Sheffield S11 8YP (Tel. 0742–587–120)

Women's Advisory Committee
TUC
Congress House
Great Russell Street
London WC1B 3LS

Women and Education Newsletter Collective
14 St. Brendan's Road
Withington
Manchester 20

INDEX